Patchworking

A Quilt Design & Coloring Book

Patchworking
A Quilt Design & Coloring Book

Judith LaBelle and Carol Ann Waugh

NEW CENTURY PUBLISHERS, INC.

Printing Code

11   12   13   14   15   16

Library of Congress Cataloging in Publication Data

Larsen, Judith LaBelle
    Patchworking: a quilt design and coloring book.
    1. Quilting—Patterns. 2. Patchwork—Patterns. I. Waugh, Carol. II. Title.
TT835.L343   1982   746.9′7041   82-14470
ISBN 0-8329-0250-0

To Marilyn Bouldin—my sister,
my inspiration, my soul-mate

Carol Ann Waugh

Contents

Acknowledgments

We owe special thanks to many people who contributed their time and talents to the writing of this book . . .

Tony Capato, who developed the computer program to generate all of the yardage charts. Without his timely help—this book would never have been finished on time!

Henry Hinz, a New York City cab driver who rescued our manuscript from the streets of New York and went out of his way to return it to us.

Mike Robbins, a stranger in Central Park who helped Henry locate us to return the lost manuscript.

Ludmillar Goldberg, whose original coloring of the design "Harlequin" appears in our book, and to her community friends for their support on that sunny summer day.

And all of our friends and relatives who gave us their understanding as we were working night and day to finish the book on time!

Patchworking

A Quilt Design & Coloring Book

1
Introduction

Quilt making has become an ever more exciting art form in recent years, as quilt makers have moved beyond "traditional" patchwork designs and begun creating totally original designs—expressions of their feelings about their own lives and experiences.

Our approach to quilt making has always been to emphasize that each and every quilt is a personal statement by the quilt maker. As we illustrated in our first book, *The Patchwork Quilt Design & Coloring Book*, the choice of color and fabric can turn even the most traditional patchwork pattern into something quite new and different.

Our purpose in this book is to illustrate how designs from widely varying sources outside the quilt making tradition can be used to create strikingly original and beautiful quilts. The designs which are included in this book were suggested by stained glass windows, Indian textiles, Chinese latticework, mosaic tiles, North African carpets, art deco, and other sources. We have adapted the styles and motifs of these divergent sources to create 50 quilt top designs. Each design is presented with a suggested use of colors and a grid which allows you to experiment with your own color scheme. By combining the quilt top and border of your own choice with your personal selection of colors and fabrics, you can create a quilt which is truly a work of art.

How to use this book   Each of the designs in this book may be used to create a quilt which will fit a standard mattress—full, queen or king. The large grids in chapter 4 cover the mattress portion of the quilt. The smaller grids in chapter 5 are border designs which you will add to the quilt top to allow for overhang on the sides and bottom and to allow for pillows at the top of your bed. Each quilt also has a frame of fabric which sets the quilt top apart from the borders. **1**

In order to make any quilt in this book, the first step is to turn to the color section which explains how color can affect design. Understanding a few basic principles of color use will help you achieve the overall effect you are looking for. Of course, we always encourage experimentation. Sometimes the best way to design a quilt is to get out your colored markers and color away!

After you have picked a pleasing design from the quilt tops in chapter 4, turn to the border section in chapter 5 and choose a border that compliments the quilt top. You can color it in the same colors as the quilt top or try new ones for a different look. Once you have selected the quilt top and border designs, choose a color for the frame and corner pieces. Now you are ready to begin the steps which lead to a finished masterpiece.

Using the charts next to each grid, determine the number of each different template code. If you have the same colors in both the quilt top and the borders, add templates with the same code and color together. Go to the "Yardage Charts" chapter beginning on page 210 and look up the required yardage for each color and template code. Add in the fabric required for the frame and corners.

If you have designed a quilt or border that is different from the one in the book, turn to the "Designing Your Own" chapter beginning on page 202 and follow the instructions to determine the number and size of the required templates.

After you have purchased your fabric, turn to the "Template" chapter beginning on page 207 and make the required template patterns. Cut out the templates and begin piecing your quilt top and borders together. Then make the quilt backing, buy the batting and sew all three pieces together. Either tie or hand stitch the quilt, finish the edges, and you are done!

All these steps are explained in detail in the "Construction" chapter beginning on page 8, where we give you step-by-step instructions on making a quilt—from the design to the last finishing touch.

2
Color

Most of us use color intuitively. We feel that we know what "works" or what we like, even though we cannot explain why. For example, we think that one combination of colors is stimulating and another uninteresting. And, in fact, there are differences—both psychological and emotional —in the way in which each of us responds to color.

Yet there are certain principles of color theory which can help you choose colors for your quilt design. The introduction to these principles, which is provided in this chapter, will help you begin to think about color in a more disciplined way and to understand how you are using—or could use—different colors or combinations of colors to effect the overall design of your quilt or to change the way in which one particular fabric is perceived.

The basic tool—the color wheel

A basic tool in understanding colors and the way they interact is the color wheel, which is illustrated on the following page. Referring to it often as you read this chapter will help you understand the principles presented.

The primary colors are red, yellow and blue. (This is the only principle of color that most of us remember from our junior high art classes!) These three colors are termed primary because each is pure (it does not contain any other color), and all other colors are created by mixing the primary colors in various proportions.

The secondary colors are created by mixing two adjacent primary colors in equal proportions. Red and yellow make orange; yellow and blue make green; blue and red make violet.

The tertiary colors are created by mixing equal porportions of a primary color and either of its secondary colors. Blue and green create blue–green and so on.

3

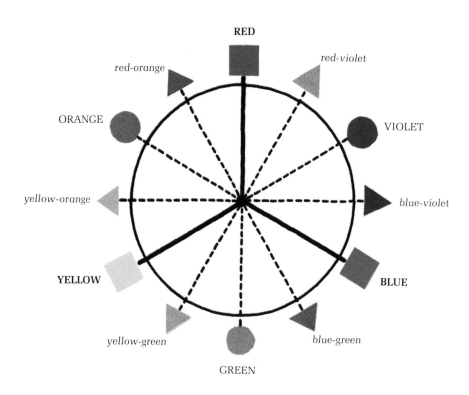

Compliments intensify   Colors which are opposite each other on the color wheel are compliments or complementary colors. Blue and orange, for example, are complimentary colors. When used together, complimentary colors make each other appear more intense. (Recently we went shopping for flowers in a market where shoppers can select individual flowers to make their own bouquets. One woman had mixed deep blue irises with bright orange African daisies to create a bouquet which drew compliments and admiring glances from many other shoppers. No doubt unknowingly, she had done a splendid job of mixing complimentary colors—making each seem even brighter and richer than it would have alone.) This effect is illustrated below:

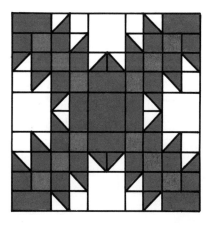

Some like it hot   We speak of colors as being either "warm" or "cool" because they seem to have different temperatures. No doubt at some time you have walked into a room decorated with shades of blue and felt that the room was cold and perhaps even unwelcoming. This is because blues as well as greens and violets (the secondary colors created with blue) are cool colors. Red, yellow and orange, on the other hand, feel warm. This difference in apparent temperature is illustrated by the "cool" green figure at the right and the "warm" yellow figure at the left of the following illustration:

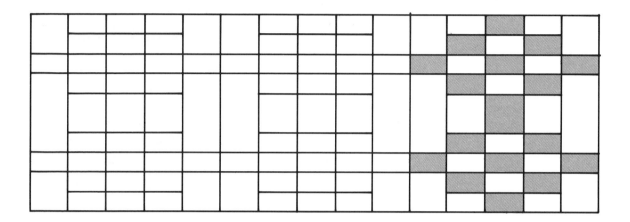

Values   The value of a color is its relative lightness or darkness. A pure color does not contain any white or black. By mixing white or black with a pure color we can create a range of values for that color. Note that this changes the value of the color but not the color itself, even though we may have names for the different values of a color. Pink, for example, is a lighter value of red.

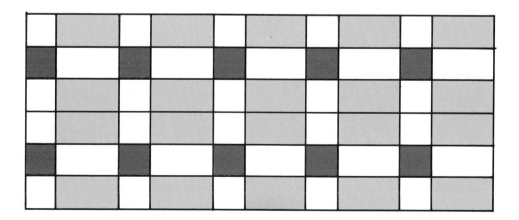

The monochromatic color scheme created by using several values of one color can be very pleasing as illustrated in the following example.

Note that by placing the extremes of a color's values next to each other, the contrast will heighten the value of each.

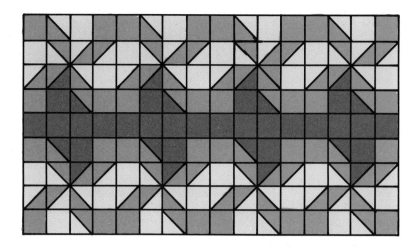

Weight   Light colors appear to be just that—light, as having little weight. Dark colors appear to be dense, heavier. Note the difference created in the design in the following illustration by changing the location of the dark and light colors.

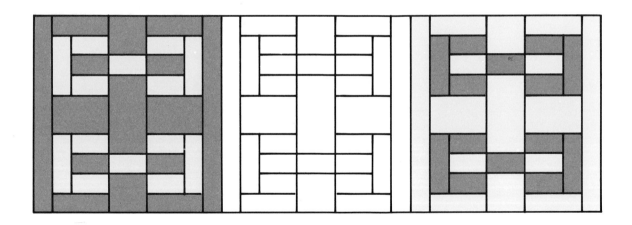

Grounds for design   The various principles introduced above can be very helpful when deciding which colors you want to have dominate your quilt design, how to intensify some colors and modulate others. By applying these principles you can also create a three-dimensional quality in your design. For example, since light colors appear to have less weight, they advance or seem to float at or above the surface of the quilt. Dark colors, which appear to be heavier, recede. Thus, if you want an area of your quilt to seem to rise above the rest, use a very light color in that area.

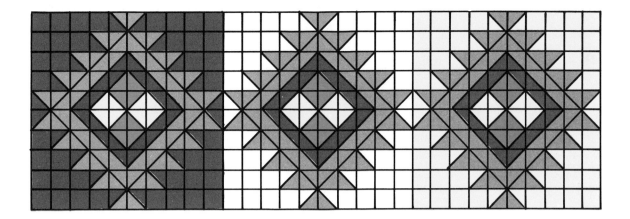

This may explain the propensity of many early American quilt makers to use a white background. A field of white made all the other colors seem very clear and intense and emphasized the design of the block used. The Amish quilters, in contrast, often created bold, geometric designs set against very dark backgrounds. The contrast with the dark backgound gave the other colors a lively quality which prevented the overall effect of the quilt from being somber or heavy.

3
Construction

Quilt making consists of 9 basic steps, each of which requires its own equipment, materials and techniques, as explained in this chapter.

Step 1: Designing

Designing a quilt is a personal matter. Besides choosing colors for your quilt, you also want to choose a design that is pleasing. The first thing to consider is how you intend to use the quilt. Are you going to use it on a bed? What is the decor of the room where the quilt will be displayed? Do you want a modern look—or something antique? How much time do you want to spend on the project—a week—several months? Answering these questions first will ensure that your finished quilt will be something you will love for years to come—not something stuck in the closet because it is never completed or doesn't quite fit!

If you are going to make a quilt for covering a bed, the most important consideration is the final measurement. You don't want the quilt to drag on the floor because you made it too long! Today's beds are made in standard sizes, but it is always wise to check the measurements of your bed to make sure that your quilt will fit.

Following are the standard mattress sizes and the quilt measurements (which allow for the overhang and pillow tuck) on which this book is based:

	Full	Queen	King
Mattress Measurement (W/L)	54″ × 75″	60″ × 80″	72″ × 84″
Quilt Measurement (W/L)	98″ × 112″	104″ × 117″	116″ × 121″

Each of the grids in this book is based on an overall design covering the mattress top. Each grid was drawn using a pattern of squares. By varying the size of the square, you can change the size of the finished quilt. For instance, in order to make a quilt top to cover the mattress for a queen size bed, you divide the width of 60 inches by a number that also divides equally into the length of 80 inches. This number could be 10 or 20. We used the number 10 and the grid for the queen size mattress measures 6 squares across the top and 8 squares down the side—each square measuring 10 inches by 10 inches. The full size is made with 9 inch squares and the king size is made with 12 inch squares.

Since quilts must be bigger than the mattress measurement, to allow for overhang on three sides and room for the pillow tuck, we have included borders which are added on all four sides in order to bring the finished quilt to standard size.

Because you may want your finished quilt either to display on a wall or to use on the bed, we have developed the following pattern so that your finished quilt will suit either purpose. This pattern results in a quilt which has measurements which are slightly different than a standard quilt, but the difference can be taken up in a pillow tuck when the quilt is placed on a bed.

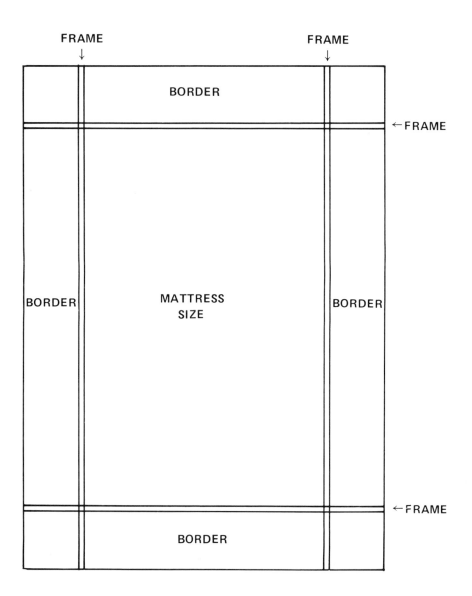

By varying the size for each element (the measurement of each square in the quilt top, the width of the frame and the width of the borders), you can make any size quilt. Here are the dimensions for the three standard quilt sizes in the book:

	Quilt top	Square size	Frame width	Corners	Border width	Finished quilt size
Full	54″ × 72″	9″	4″	18″ × 18″	18″	96″ × 116″
Queen	60″ × 80″	10″	2″	20″ × 20″	20″	104″ × 124″
King	72″ × 96″	12″	4″	18″ × 18″	18″	116″ × 140″

You can see by the above finished quilt measurements that the full and queen size are fairly close to the standard quilt sizes—the only difference being the length, which is slightly longer. But the difference can be made up by tucking the quilt more deeply under the pillows so that the border shows in its entirety across the top of the bed. The king size is quite a bit longer and you can choose to eliminate the border at the top of the quilt in order to reduce the work, but we suggest you go to the extra trouble so your quilt can be used on the wall as well as the bed.

If you decide to make a quilt using our suggested colors (or if you choose the same design but alter the color combination by replacing red with blue, green with yellow, etc.), you can use the template charts in this book to determine the size and number of templates needed to complete the part of the quilt which covers the mattress top. The same procedure goes for the borders in the book. A good rule to remember when determining how much time you might want to spend on the quilt is that the more pieces you have to cut and sew together, the longer it will take you to complete the quilt. Here is an idea of how much time is involved:

Up to 500 pieces:	1–2 weeks
500 to 1000 pieces:	3–5 weeks
Over 1000:	several months

If you decide to change the design and create something completely new, turn to the "Designing Your Own" chapter beginning on page 202 to determine the template sizes and number.

In either case, however, you will want to experiment with color in order to develop a color scheme that gives you the results you want. We use medium-tipped colored markers that you can purchase in any art supply store. You can either color directly in the book, photocopy several pages from the book and try out your colors on these pages, or use tracing paper over the designs and color on that. We recommend that you photocopy the grids so you can try out several different color combinations.

Once you have determined the color scheme and design for the part of the quilt that covers the mattress, you'll want to choose a border that compliments the quilt top. Turn to the "Border" chapter beginning on page 120 and go through the same process. A good way to see if you like a border with the top is to place the border next to the top and see the results. (Of course, when you do this the border will look much bigger than it will after you sew it because the scale of the charts is different, but it will give you some idea of what the combination will be like.)

Now that you have chosen the quilt top and border, the only remaining choice is the color for the fabric frame and corners. We prefer to leave the corners plain instead of pieced and use hand-quilting patterns to add more interest to the quilt. But you can use a pieced design, either from the quilt top or from the borders.

If you have chosen a design from this book, the next step is to determine how much fabric you need to buy of each color.

Simply take the chart for the quilt top and the chart for the borders and put them together by color and template code. Add together the same color and template code as in the following example:

Quilt Top Chart			Border Chart		
Color	Number	Code	Color	Number	Code
Yellow	135	R1	Yellow	28	R1
Blue	45	T16	Blue	30	T7
	20	S3		150	S3
Green	250	S7	Brown	80	S7
	25	R25		20	R25

When you add the same colors and template codes together, you should have the following chart:

Color	Number	Code
Yellow	163	R1
Blue	30	T7
	45	T16
	170	S3
Green	250	S7
	25	R25
Brown	80	S7
	20	R25

Turn to the yardage charts beginning on page 210 and determine the number of yards of fabric for each color to purchase for the quilt top and borders.

The final step in the process—before you buy your fabric—is to add in the necessary yardage for the frame and corners. Since this is always the same amount, we've figured out the yardage for you. When you cut out the frames, simply measure the number of inches in the width and add the seam allowance of ⅜ inch on each side and tear strips of fabric —selvage to selvage—until you reach the required number of strips.

Quilt Size	Frame	Corners
Full	2.0 yards (36″ or 45″)	2.25 yards (36″) 1.25 yards (45″)
Queen	1.5 yards (36″ or 45″)	2.25 yards (36″) 1.25 yards (45″)
King	2.5 yards (36″ or 45″)	2.25 yards (36″) 1.25 yards (45″)

Step 2: Fabric selection

After you have designed your quilt and determined the number of yards of each of the different fabrics you will need to make the quilt, it's time to go to the fabric store and buy the fabric.

The variety of materials available today can be bewildering. 100% cotton fabrics or cotton and polyester blends are generally the best choice for patchwork. Choose materials that you would use for making a blouse or dress. These will be pliable yet have enough body. Remember that the design of the quilt may influence your choice of fabrics. The smaller and more irregular the pieces are, the more important it is that the fabric have a firm weave which will help prevent it from shifting or stretching out of shape. A firm weave will also help avoid fraying and pulling at the seams as the quilt is used and cleaned. All of the fabrics used for the quilt should be roughly the same in weight and texture.

Step 3: Preparing the fabric

A splendid quilt may be ruined when it is cleaned unless the fabric was carefully prepared when the quilt was made. So before you begin making your quilt, be sure to wash the fabric. This will allow you to test for color-fastness and to make sure that if the fabric is going to shrink, it shrinks *before* it is cut and sewn into the quilt top.

After washing the fabric, iron it carefully. You will have problems making the pieces match properly if the fabric has wrinkles which smooth open while you are sewing the pieces together. Some quilters spray the fabric with starch while ironing to help stiffen it so that it holds its shape and is easier to work with.

Piecing the fabric will also be easier if the grain of the fabric is straight, that is the vertical and horizontal threads (the warp and the weft) cross at right angles.

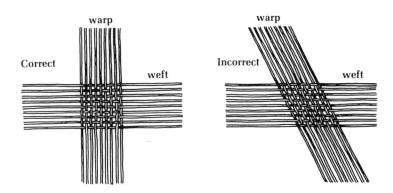

If the grain is straight the fabric is less likely to stretch out of shape and pucker at the seams.

To check whether the grain is straight, fold the fabric in half with the selvage edges together. Holding the fabric at the folded edge, let the edges hang. If the grain is straight, the cut edges will hang evenly. If the edges are not even, straighten the grain by holding the fabric with one hand on each selvage and gently stretch it diagonally. Continue pulling gently until the edges hang evenly. (Be sure to check frequently so that you don't overdo it!)

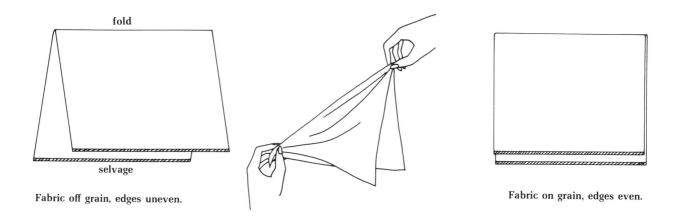

fold

selvage

Fabric off grain, edges uneven.

Fabric on grain, edges even.

Step 4: Cutting the fabric

This is the part of the quilting process which we enjoy the least, yet it is one which may cause you the most problems if it is not done properly. We recommend that each template be traced and cut separately. While this takes more time, the accuracy that results will reduce your piecing problems later. And since you will be using the cut edge of the template as your seam indicator, it is extremely important that each template size is exact.

After you make your template pattern (see the "Template" chapter beginning on page 207 for instructions), smooth the prepared fabric open on a hard flat surface, wrong side up. Be sure to place each template with at least one side along the warp or weft—the straight grain of the fabric. (See the "Yardage Charts" chapter beginning on page 210 for helpful hints on laying out the templates on the fabric to get the most pieces from the yardage.)

Using a sharp pencil or an indelible felt marker, trace around each template keeping the point of the marking instrument slanted toward the template so that the outline of the template is traced as accurately as possible. As you trace one template next to the other, be sure to leave about 1/4 inch between each one so that any inaccuracy in cutting or tracing of one template will not affect the other.

When cutting out the templates from the fabric, be sure to use sharp, clean scissors. We recommend using scissors with at least a 4-inch blade which you use only for cutting fabric.

Step 5: Piecing

All of the designs in this book can be pieced together by machine. This means that only straight seams are required and no template must be pieced around a corner. When you first look at your completed design, it may be difficult to see where to start since most of the designs are not repetitive blocks (as in traditional quilt designs) where you sew together each block first and then piece the blocks together. So here are a few tips on piecing together an overall design.

Quilts are generally pieced together by using one of two methods (or a combination of both):

1. *Strip piecing:* This method is used when your design divides itself into strips—either vertically or horizontally. If you can see a continuous seam running across or down the top, you can piece together that portion

of the quilt using the strip method. A good example of a quilt that should be pieced together this way is the "Navajo Necklace" on page 96.

When using the strip technique, start from one end of the strip and piece each piece together in sequence until you finish the strip. Continue piecing each strip of the quilt and then piece the strips together in sequence until the entire quilt top is completed.

2. Block piecing: This method is used when your design divides itself into natural blocks. In some cases, each block will be a different size. Generally, it's a good idea to start with the most complicated portion of your quilt top by breaking down each block into smaller blocks and piecing the smaller blocks together first. Just remember that your piecing should be done so that all your seams result in straight seam piecing—not corners. Otherwise, you will have to piece some blocks together by hand. If your design contains triangles, be sure that you piece each triangle together first so that you are actually piecing squares. A good example of a quilt that should be pieced together using the block technique is the "Cat's Whiskers" on page 80. When using the block technique, piece together all the blocks and then sew the blocks together until you complete the quilt top.

The thread used for piecing the top may be either #50 mercerized cotton thread or cotton-wrapped polyester. Either kind is widely available in many colors, but you can use one color for all of the piecing. Choose a color that will blend with the various fabrics you will be using.

If the design which you are making has many small pieces, you can save time by sewing pairs of pieces together without cutting the thread between each piece. Allow an inch or so of thread between each pair for the thread to be cut later. The twisting of the threads, and the fact that you will be seaming across each of the edges, will be sufficient to prevent the seams from unraveling.

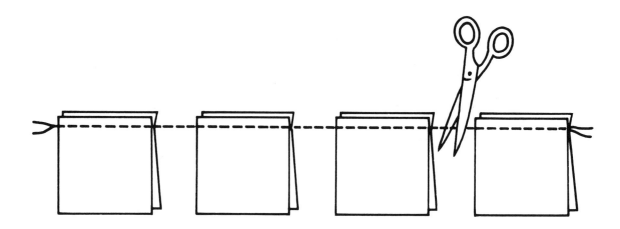

Each seam should be pressed before you sew across it while making another seam. Generally you should press seams flat and to one side. It is best not to press open the seams unless several seams will come together, then you may want to press the seams open to avoid bulkiness. For the same reason, you should press joining seams in opposite directions.

When light and dark pieces are seamed together, press the seam toward the dark piece so that the seam allowance will not show through your finished quilt top.

Press each seam first on the back of the piece and then on the front. Using a steam iron will give a nice, crisp finish.

Step 6: Putting it together

Your finished quilt will be composed of the quilt top (mattress covering, frames, borders and corners), a filling and a lining.

The lining, or backing, may be made from any fabric which is complimentary in color and weight to the quilt top. The lining fabric must also be washed and pressed. If you use a large sheet, you can avoid seaming the lining.

The kind of filling which you use will affect the amount of quilting which you must do to hold it in place. The cotton batting used in many old quilts would shift and become lumpy with use so the quilting stitches were usually no more than 2 inches apart.

Most quilters today use polyester batting which is available in large quilt sizes. Polyester batting is glazed so that it holds its shape and the fibers do not work their way through the quilting holes or seams. Because the batting is more stable, the lines of quilting may be further apart. Three inches is a fairly common width.

Prepare the quilt top by sewing together all of the pieces (the top, frame, borders and corners). Prepare the lining and the batting by sewing together fabric or batting to measure the same width and length as the quilt top.

After you have prepared all three elements, place the lining right side down on a clean, smooth surface. Cover the lining with the batting and cover both with the quilt top placed right side up. Smooth all of the layers. Use several large safety pins to fasten the layers together so they do not shift. Next, hand-baste the layers together using a long straight stitch. Working from the center out, form a pattern either like a checkerboard or the spokes of a wheel.

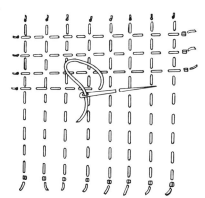 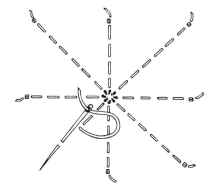

Step 7: Quilting

It is possible to quilt by machine as well as by hand. Although we are all in favor of piecing the quilt by machine, we would urge you to do your quilting by hand. Very few of us are proficient enough in handling bulky materials on the sewing machine to obtain the intended results. More importantly, the soft definition provided by hand-quilted lines adds greatly to both the visual and tactile texture of the finished quilt.

Hand-quilting involves only one simple stitch—a fine running stitch. Of course the fineness and regularity of this stitch is very important. Many quilters find that they can control the stitch better if they work with one hand below the quilt to guide the needle. Experiment and find the technique that suits you best.

Many quilters today do not have sufficient space to use the traditional quilting frame on which the entire quilt is stretched out. (This type of frame is familiar from pictures of quilting bees which show several women working on the quilt at the same time.) So manufacturers have made smaller versions which roll up, so that only a small portion of the quilt is accessible. And for those very small apartments, there are quilting hoops—some of which are on stands—which you use like an embroidery hoop and stretch a section at a time as you work. Whichever type of frame you use, your quilting should be done from the center of the quilt out to the edge.

The easiest way to quilt is to outline each piece with a row of stitching about ⅜ of an inch on each side of the seam. This outline stitch emphasizes the pieced design and allows you to avoid marking the quilt with an outline for a more intricate design. However, if the design which you have chosen has large templates (5-inch squares or larger), outline quilting may not be sufficient to hold the lining in place. You could add rows of stitches parallel to those of your outline quilting. But you may decide to add more visual interest to your quilt (especially in the corners) by using a more intricate quilting design. Stencils for traditional designs such as scrolls and feathers can be purchased from quilting shops or through catalogs, or you may wish to create your own designs.

Whatever design you use, you must mark the quilt with the design before stitching. It is best to use dressmaker's chalk, carbon or pencil, to make sure that the markings come off when you clean the quilt. If you mark with pencil, be sure to do it lightly and use fine dots rather than a straight line since this is the most difficult type of marking to remove from the finished quilt.

You may also want to try using quilting thread which is available in most sewing stores. It is strong, smooth and resists knotting.

Wool bats may either be too bulky to quilt or so thin that they do not need to be closely quilted to prevent lumping. So if you are using a wool bat you may want to tie the layers of the quilt together rather than hand sewing it.

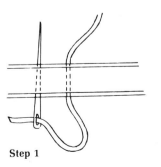

Step 1

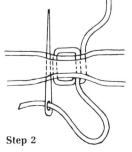

Step 2

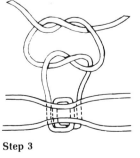

Step 3

To use the tying method, spread the layers of the quilt as described previously and pin together. Use chalk to mark the spots to be tied. (These marks should be no more than 7 to 8 inches apart.) Double thread a tapestry needle (which has a large eye) with yarn or heavy decorative thread. Leaving about 2 inches of yarn or thread above the quilt, take two stitches in the same spot. Firmly tie two knots and trim the yarn to an even length.

Step 8: Finishing the edges

The edges of your quilt can be finished in several ways. You may fold a narrow edge of the lining over the top of quilt or a narrow edge of the top of the quilt over the lining. We recommend that you fold the lining over the top since this will create an additional narrow border framing the quilt. Either way, turn under the raw edge and hem by hand. The folding and hemming must be done carefully so that the material which is folded over forms a straight, even band of color around the edge of the quilt. If you prefer not to have any contrasting band of color on either the top or the lining, fold the raw edges of the top and the lining to the center and overcast the edge.

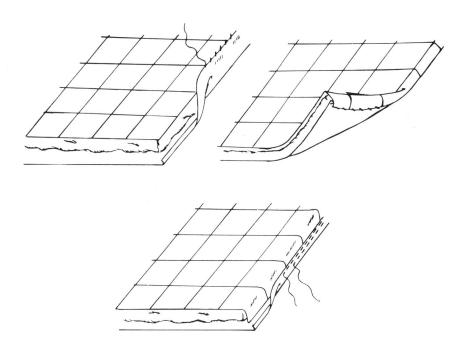

Step 9: The final touch

Your quilt will be a work of art. Just as a painter signs and dates her work, we suggest that you sign and date your quilt by stitching your name and the date on the front or the back. Some early American quilters also indicated the date that they began their quilts. Perhaps you can take heart from the fact that even they sometimes took several years to complete a quilt!

4
50 New Quilt Designs

Good design lasts through the ages, crosses cultural and religious barriers and stays with us in many different forms. As we researched this book, we came across many design motifs repeated in various art forms from different cultures at different periods in history. So while each grid is unique, you may find some elements of a grid which seem familiar, such as triangles set on their corners to form a flowerlike shape.

Just keeping an open mind to the possible sources of designs will help you discover the possibility of drawing quilt designs from many new and exciting sources, including those from which we have drawn inspiration, such as stained glass windows, mosaic tiles, Indian textiles, iron grill-work and even graffito!

We have taken the liberty of naming our original color suggestions. We hope you enjoy doing the same for the designs you create!

Index

Sky Plane

Color	Number of templates	Template Codes		
		Full	Queen	King
Beige	4	R57	R68	R78
	2	R59	R70	R80
	2	R135	R138	R141
Brown	2	R5	R16	R32
	4	R59	R70	R80
	4	R57	R68	R78
Green	2	S24	S25	S26
	6	R57	R68	R78
	2	R59	R70	R80
White	2	R99	R108	R116
	2	R130	R132	R139
	2	R131	R133	R140
Blue	4	R50	R62	R72
	4	R57	R68	R78
	4	R59	R70	R80
	8	R102	R111	R119
Total	54			

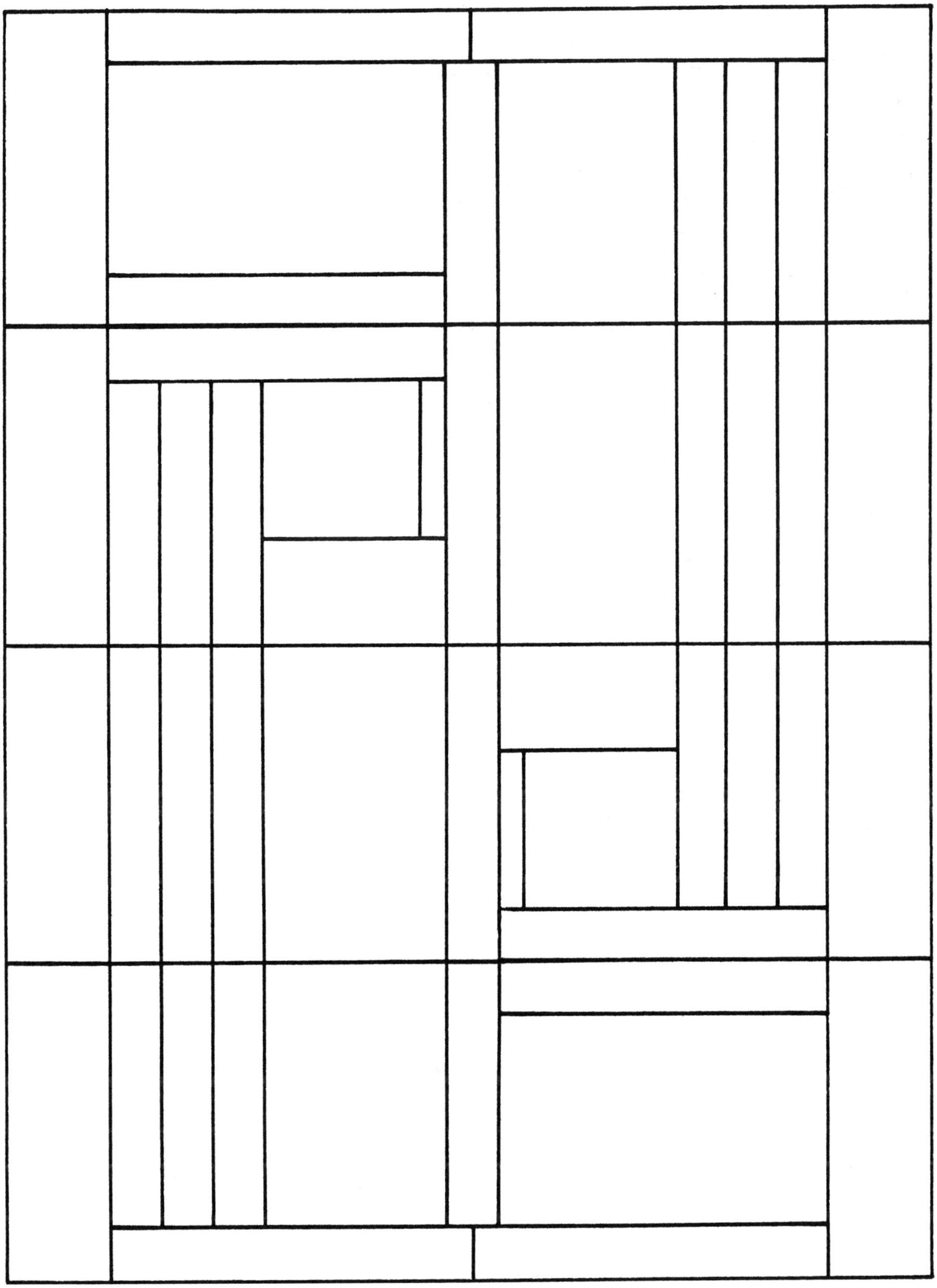

Pinwheel Star

Color	Number of templates	Template Codes		
		Full	Queen	King
White	4	S24	S25	S26
	16	T31	T32	T34
Red	4	T23	T26	T30
	28	T31	T32	T34
Black	12	S24	S25	S26
	4	T23	T26	T30
	16	T31	T32	T34
Total	84			

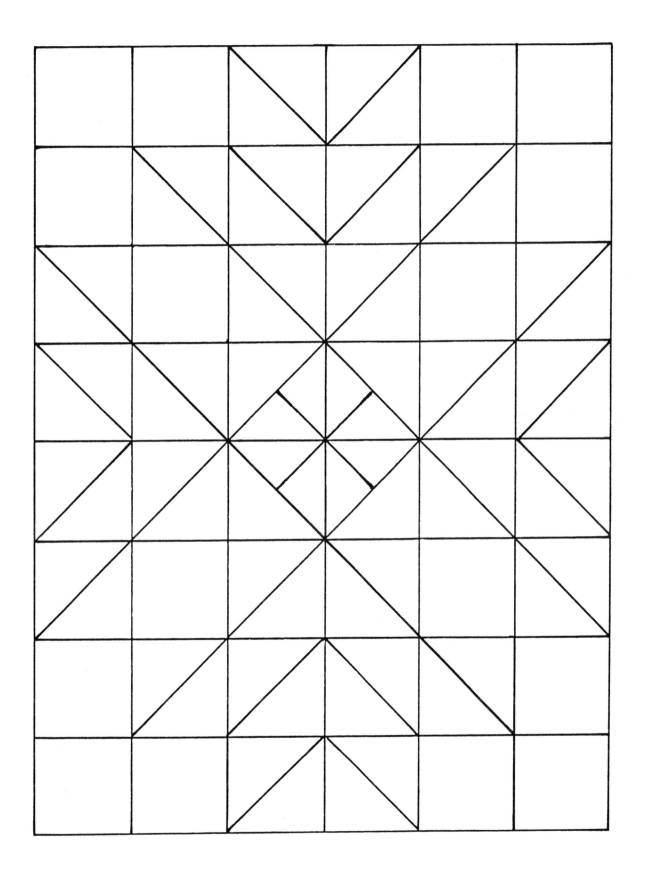

23

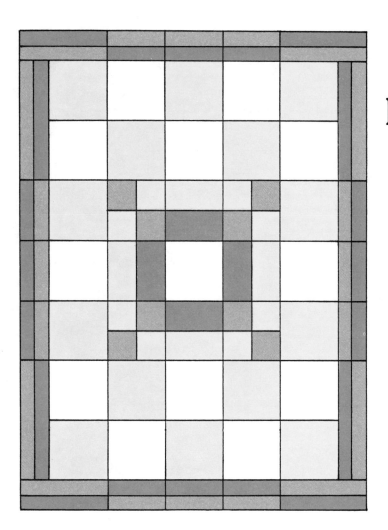

El Baño

| | | | Template Codes | |
Color	Number of templates	Full	Queen	King
White	1	S24	S25	S26
Yellow	8	S13	S15	S17
	14	S24	S25	S26
	4	R83	R90	R100
Blue	12	R41	R46	R55
	4	R42	R47	R59
	4	R43	R48	R60
	4	R83	R90	R100
Green	8	S13	S15	S17
	12	R41	R46	R55
	4	R42	R47	R59
	4	R43	R48	R60
Total	**91**			

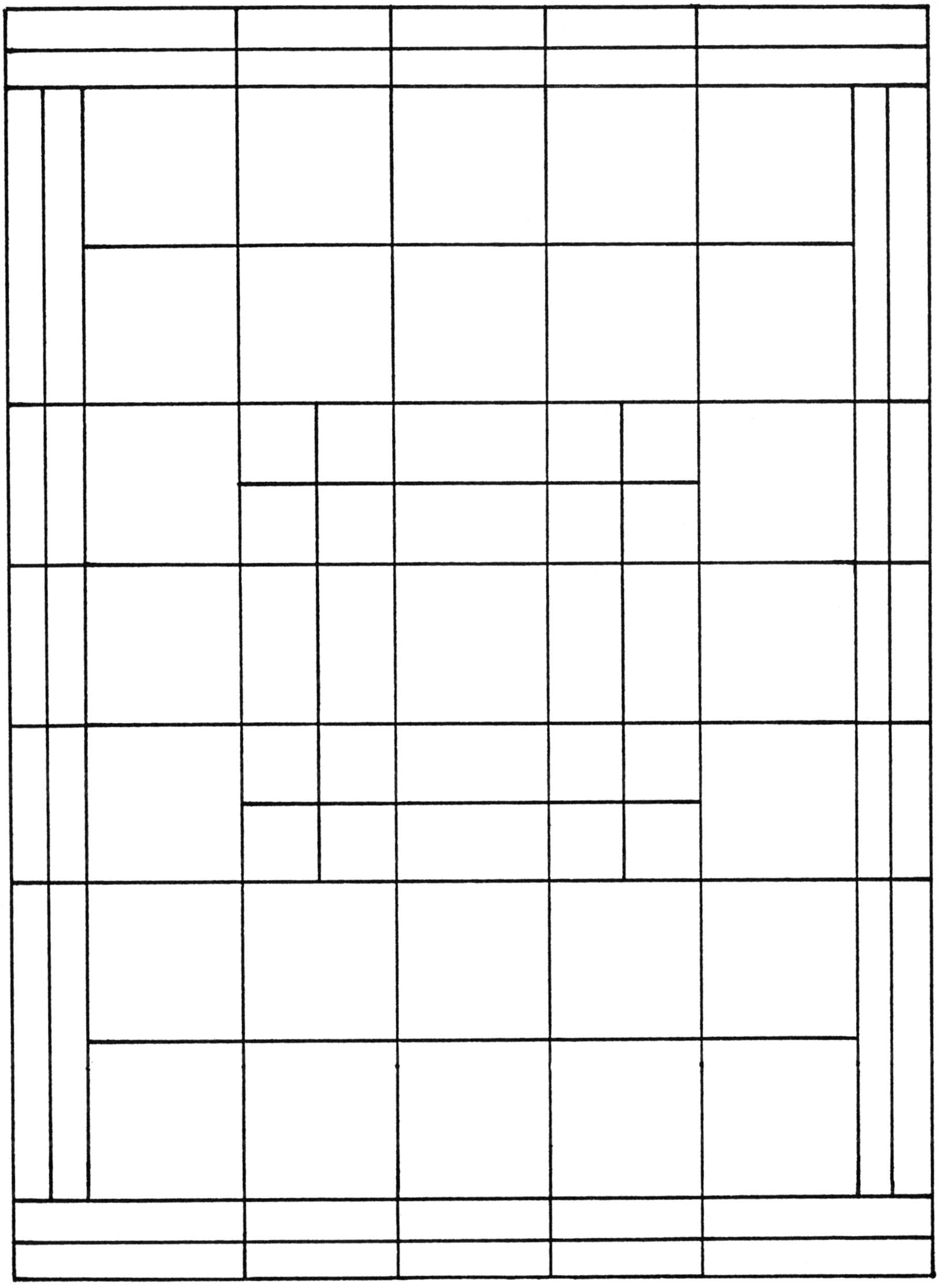

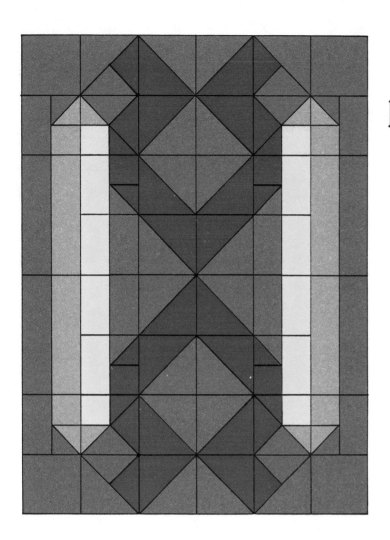

Hot Gothic

Color	Number of templates	Template Codes Full	Queen	King
Blue	8	T23	T26	T30
	8	T31	T32	T34
Yellow	4	S13	S15	S17
	4	R83	R90	R100
	2	R87	R94	R105
Green	8	T15	T19	T22
	4	R84	R91	R102
	2	R87	R94	R105
Pink	4	S13	S15	S17
	8	T15	T19	T22
	8	T23	T26	T30
	16	T31	T32	T34
Gray	4	S24	S25	S26
	8	T15	T19	T22
	12	T31	T32	T34
	6	R87	R94	R105
Total	**106**			

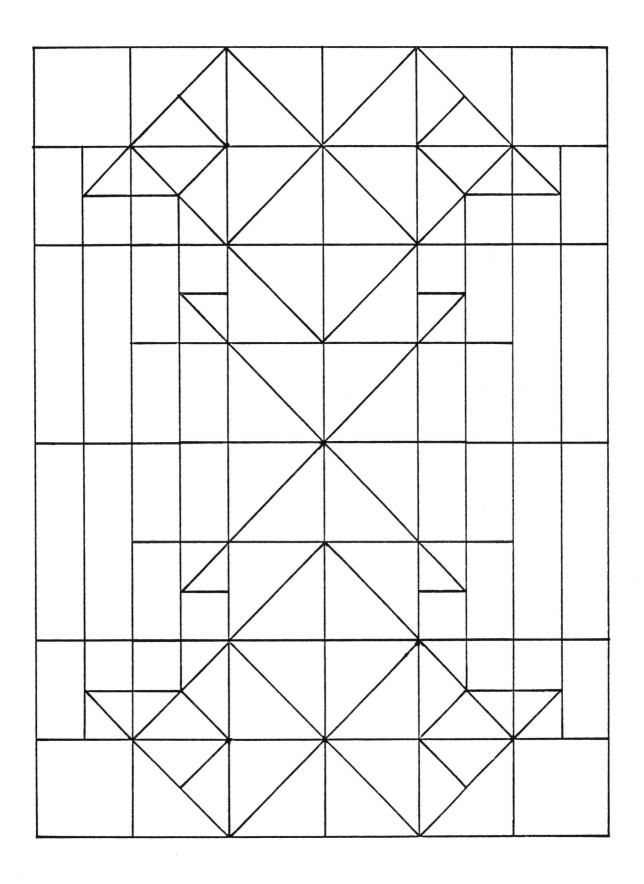

Fuchsia Fault

		Template Codes		
Color	Number of templates	Full	Queen	King
Fuchsia	2	S24	S25	S26
	2	T7	T9	T13
	8	T22	T24	T28
	2	T31	T32	T34
	6	R50	R62	R72
	6	R53	R64	R74
	20	R97	R107	R115
White	8	S24	S25	S26
	4	T7	T9	T13
	8	T22	T24	T28
	6	R50	R62	R72
	26	R53	R64	R74
	8	R97	R107	R115
Total	**110**			

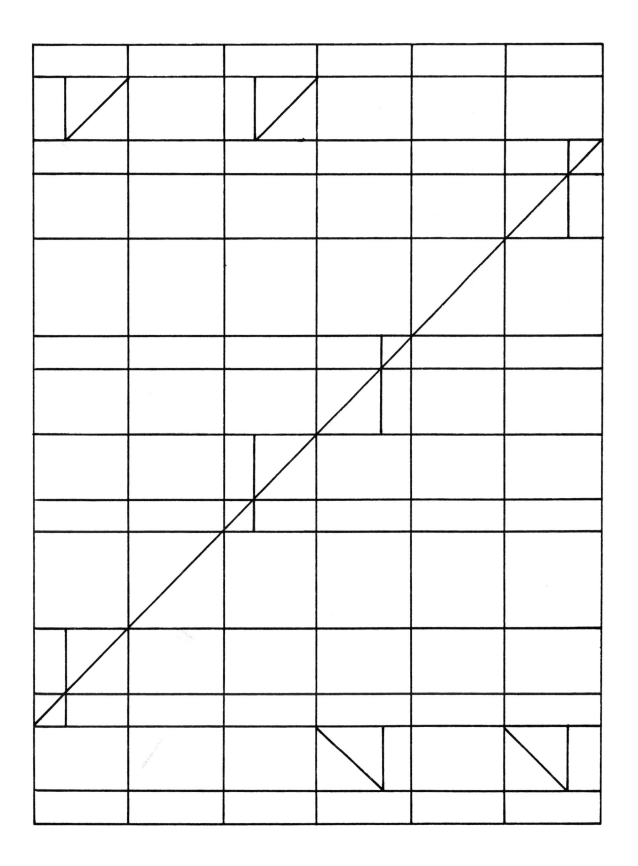

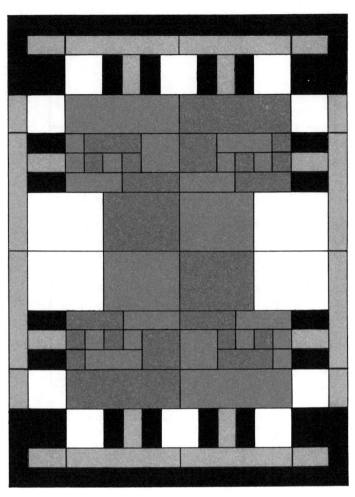

Pharaoh's Passage

| | | **Template Codes** | | |
Color	Number of templates	Full	Queen	King
White	10	S17	S19	S22
	4	R121	R126	R134
Gold	16	R50	R62	R72
	8	R59	R70	R80
Gray	10	S7	S9	S11
	2	S17	S19	S22
	6	R53	R64	R74
	2	R108	R111	R119
	2	R121	R126	R134
Turquoise	10	S7	S9	S11
	2	S17	S19	S22
	6	R53	R64	R74
	2	R108	R111	R119
	2	R121	R126	R134
Black	4	S7	S9	S11
	16	R50	R62	R72
	4	R53	R64	R74
	4	R59	R70	R80
	4	R97	R107	R115
Total	**114**			

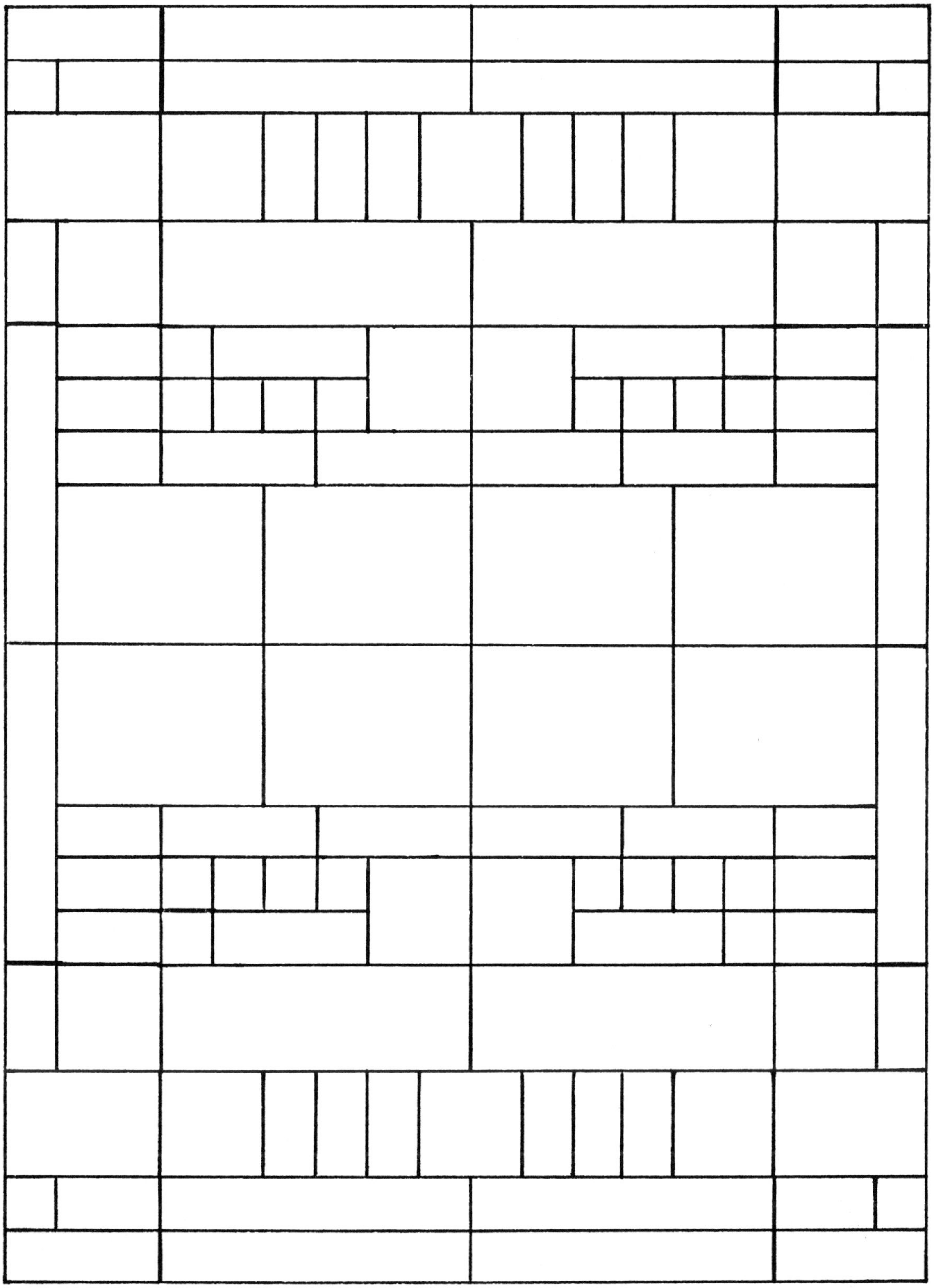

Vernal Equinox

			Template Codes	
Color	Number of templates	Full	Queen	King
Pink	20	S7	S9	S11
	20	R53	R64	R74
Green	20	S7	S9	S11
	20	R55	R66	R76
White	6	S17	S19	S22
	4	S24	S25	S26
	6	R50	R62	R72
	16	R53	R64	R74
	2	R55	R66	R76
	2	R97	R107	R115
	8	R100	R109	R117
	4	R121	R126	R134
Total	**128**			

33

Flowergirl

Color	Number of templates	Full	Template Codes Queen	King
Yellow	9	S18	S20	S23
Orange	18	S18	S20	S23
Red	2	S8	S10	S12
	18	S18	S20	S23
Green	8	S8	S10	S12
	22	S18	S20	S23
White	16	S18	S20	S23
	20	T8	T10	T14
	4	T15	T19	T22
	14	T27	T29	T32
Total	**131**			

35

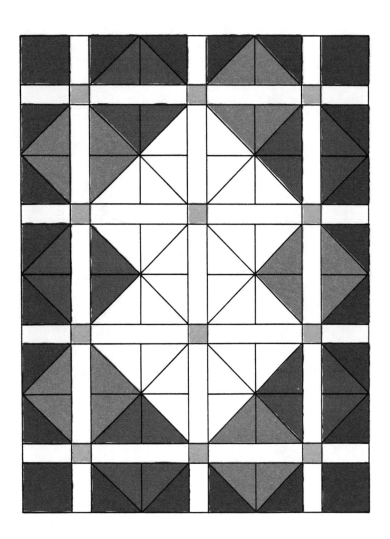

Palazzo

Color	Number of templates	Template Codes Full	Queen	King
Pink	20	T22	T24	T28
Green	20	T22	T24	T28
Yellow	12	S7	S9	S11
Brown	4	S18	S20	S23
	20	T22	T24	T28
White	28	T22	T24	T28
	14	R51	R63	R73
	17	R57	R68	R78
Total	**135**			

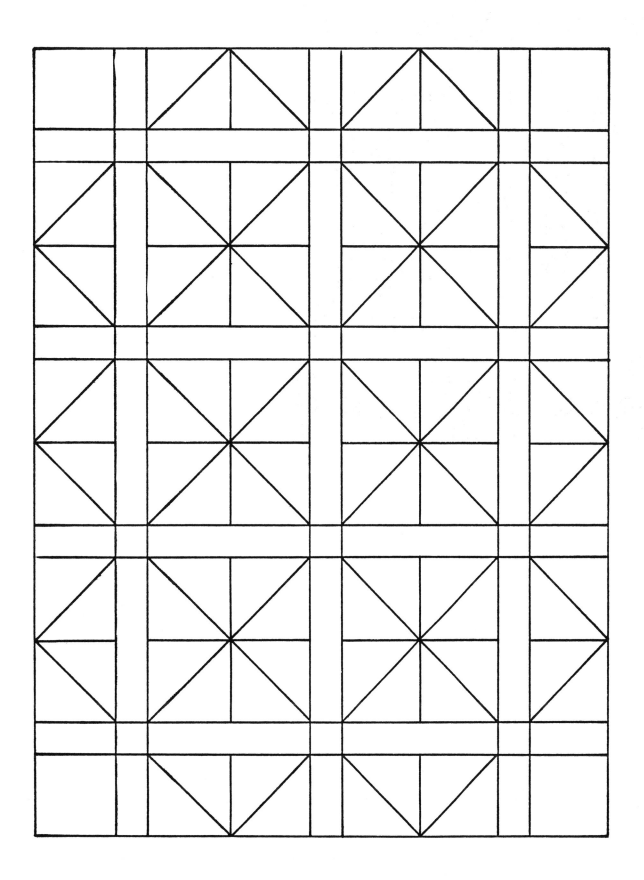

Spring Moon's Courtyard

		Template Codes		
Color	**Number of templates**	**Full**	**Queen**	**King**
Green	4	R50	R62	R72
	8	R55	R66	R76
Brown	4	S7	S9	S11
	4	R58	R69	R79
Pink	2	S7	S9	S11
	6	R50	R62	R72
	2	R55	R66	R76
Blue	2	S7	S9	S11
	6	R50	R62	R72
	2	R55	R66	R76
Orange	4	S7	S9	S11
	4	R55	R66	R76
	4	R59	R70	R80

		Template Codes		
Color	**Number of templates**	**Full**	**Queen**	**King**
Yellow	4	S7	S9	S11
	4	R53	R64	R74
	4	R58	R69	R79
Purple	12	S7	S9	S11
	12	R53	R64	R74
	6	R55	R66	R76
	4	R59	R70	R80
White	8	S7	S9	S11
	8	R50	R62	R72
	8	R55	R66	R76
	4	R57	R68	R78
	12	R59	R70	R80
Total	**138**			

Balloons Over Wheat Fields

		Template Codes		
Color	Number of templates	Full	Queen	King
Blue	36	T15	T19	T22
White	36	T15	T19	T22
Dark Brown	32	T15	T19	T22
Yellow	16	T15	T19	T22
	4	T31	T32	T34
	4	R83	R90	R100
	4	R124	R129	R137
Orange	4	S24	S25	S26
	8	T15	T19	T22
	4	T31	T32	T34
	4	R42	R47	R59
	4	R83	R90	R100
	4	R124	R129	R137
Total	160			

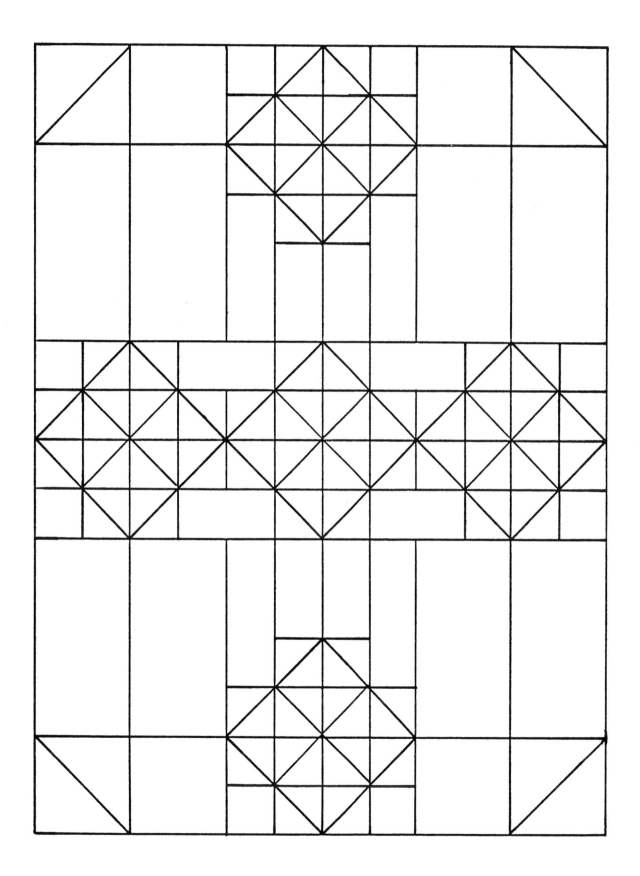

41

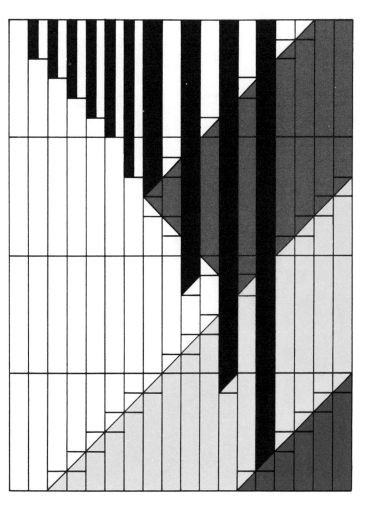

Recession

Color	Number of templates	Template Codes Full	Queen	King
Blue	1	S7	S9	S11
	6	T7	T9	T13
	1	R50	R62	R72
	1	R53	R64	R74
	1	R55	R66	R76
	1	R57	R68	R78
Red	1	S7	S9	S11
	14	T7	T9	T13
	3	R50	R62	R72
	1	R53	R64	R74
	2	R55	R66	R76
	2	R57	R68	R78
	4	R59	R70	R80
Yellow	4	S7	S9	S11
	20	T7	T9	T13
	4	R50	R62	R72
	3	R53	R64	R74
	3	R55	R66	R76
	2	R57	R68	R78
	7	R59	R70	R80
Black	1	S7	S9	S11

Color	Number of templates	Template Codes Full	Queen	King
	4	T7	T9	T13
	2	R3	R14	R29
	1	R5	R16	R32
	1	R7	R18	R34
	1	R9	R21	R36
	2	R11	R23	R38
	1	R50	R62	R72
	1	R55	R66	R76
	9	R59	R70	R80
White	4	S7	S9	S11
	18	T7	T9	T13
	2	R3	R14	R29
	1	R5	R16	R32
	1	R7	R18	R34
	1	R9	R21	R36
	2	R11	R23	R38
	5	R50	R62	R72
	3	R53	R64	R74
	3	R55	R66	R76
	3	R57	R68	R78
	18	R59	R70	R80
Total	**165**			

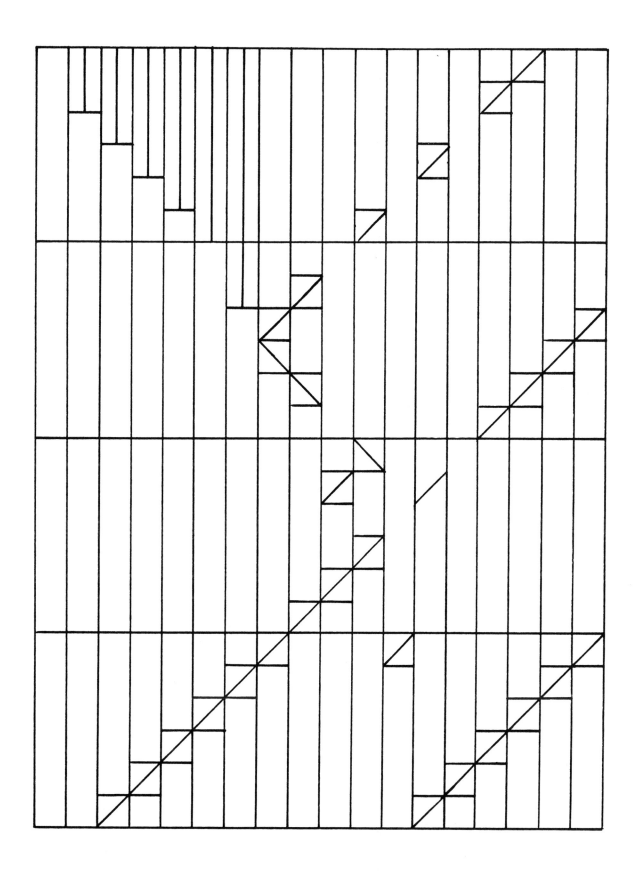

43

Galleria

		Template Codes		
Color	**Number of templates**	**Full**	**Queen**	**King**
Yellow	4	S1	S2	S3
	4	R124	R129	R137
Gold	8	R5	R16	R32
	8	R11	R23	R38
	16	R50	R62	R72
	16	R57	R68	R78
Green	8	S1	S2	S3
	16	T22	T24	T28
	16	R5	R16	R32
	16	R11	R23	R38
White	4	S1	S2	S3
	12	S7	S9	S11
	16	T22	T24	T28
	8	R5	R16	R32
	8	R11	R23	R38
	8	R53	R64	R74
Total	**168**			

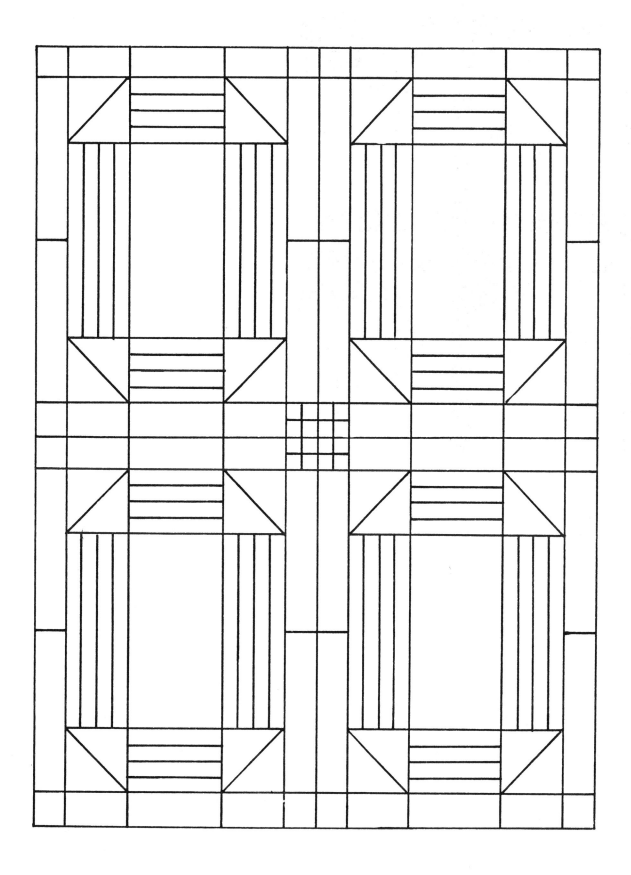

Abstraction

		Template Codes		
Color	Number of templates	Full	Queen	King
Blue	12	R54	R65	R75
Orange	8	S7	S9	S11
	4	R50	R62	R72
Red	16	R53	R64	R74
	12	R54	R65	R75
Green	4	R4	R15	R31
	8	R51	R63	R73
Brown	4	S7	S9	S11
	4	R50	R62	R72
	4	R57	R68	R78
	8	R59	R70	R80
White	40	S7	S9	S11

		Template Codes		
Color	Number of templates	Full	Queen	King
	4	R3	R14	R29
	12	R49	R61	R71
	12	R53	R64	R74
	8	R59	R70	R80
Yellow	4	S1	S2	S3
	8	R1	R12	R25
	4	R3	R14	R29
	4	R4	R15	R31
	8	R50	R62	R72
	4	R57	R68	R78
Total	192			

47

Holy Grail

		Template Codes		
Color	Number of templates	Full	Queen	King
Brown	10	R3	R14	R29
	2	R5	R16	R32
Green	8	S7	S9	S11
	12	R1	R12	R25
	2	R5	R16	R32
	8	R50	R62	R72
Orange	2	S7	S9	S11
	8	R2	R13	R29
	12	R3	R14	R27
	8	R4	R15	R31
	16	R7	R18	R34
	8	R9	R21	R36
	8	R59	R70	R80

		Template Codes		
Color	Number of templates	Full	Queen	King
Red	4	S1	S2	S3
	4	S24	S25	S26
	16	R1	R12	R25
	2	R5	R16	R32
	16	R49	R61	R71
	4	R50	R62	R72
	10	R53	R64	R74
	8	R54	R65	R75
	8	R56	R67	R77
	8	R57	R68	R78
	8	R81	R88	R96
	8	R82	R89	R98
Total	**202**			

49

Bygones

Color	Number of templates	Template Codes		
		Full	Queen	King
Red	24	R55	R66	R76
Yellow	24	R53	R64	R74
Blue	48	T7	T9	T13
	24	R53	R64	R74
White	12	S17	S19	S22
	48	T7	T9	T13
	24	R55	R66	R76
Total	**204**			

Sunrise, Sunset

		Template Codes					Template Codes		
Color	Number of templates	Full	Queen	King	Color	Number of templates	Full	Queen	King
Light Orange	12	R6	R17	R33		6	R9	R21	R36
	12	R11	R23	R38		6	R10	R22	R37
Red	6	R5	R16	R32	Pink	6	R1	R12	R25
	6	R8	R20	R35		6	R6	R17	R33
	6	R9	R21	R36		6	R7	R18	R34
Dark Blue	6	R5	R16	R32		6	R9	R21	R36
	6	R8	R20	R35		6	R10	R22	R37
	6	R9	R21	R36		6	R11	R23	R38
Orange	6	R3	R14	R29	Light Blue	6	R1	R12	R25
	18	R7	R18	R34		6	R6	R17	R33
	6	R10	R22	R37		6	R7	R18	R34
	6	R11	R23	R38		6	R9	R21	R36
Medium Blue	6	R3	R20	R35		6	R10	R22	R37
	12	R7	R18	R34		6	R11	R23	R38
	6	R8	R20	R35	Total	204			

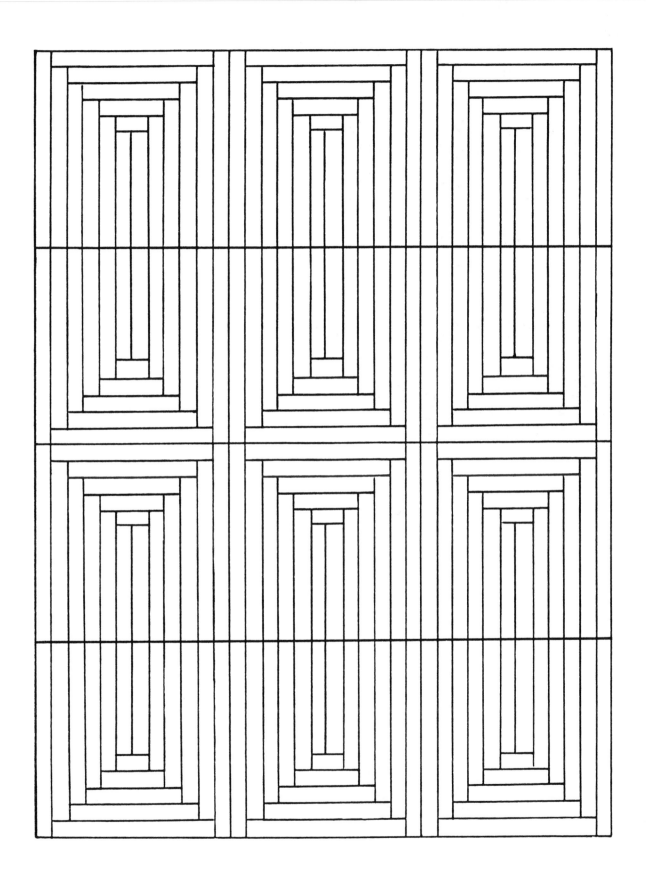

53

Canaveral

		Template Codes					Template Codes		
Color	Number of templates	Full	Queen	King	Color	Number of templates	Full	Queen	King
Blue	4	T1	T2	T3		2	R6	R17	R33
	40	T7	T9	T13		2	R10	R22	R37
	2	R8	R20	R35		4	R11	R23	R38
	2	R9	R21	R36		4	R102	R111	R119
Brown	10	T1	T2	T3	Orange	2	S7	S9	S11
	2	R2	R13	R27		4	T1	T2	T3
	4	R4	R15	R31		6	T7	T9	T13
	2	R7	R18	R34		2	R1	R12	R25
	6	R10	R22	R37		2	R5	R16	R32
	8	R11	R23	R38		2	R8	R20	R35
White	2	T27	T29	T32		2	R10	R22	R37
	4	T31	T32	T34		2	R49	R61	R71
	2	T33	T37	T38		2	R54	R65	R75
	2	R113	R121	R127		2	R58	R69	R79
	2	R123	R128	R136		2	R59	R70	R80
Turquoise	20	S7	S9	S11		8	R102	R111	R119
	2	T1	T2	T3	**Total**	**204**			
	40	T7	T9	T13					

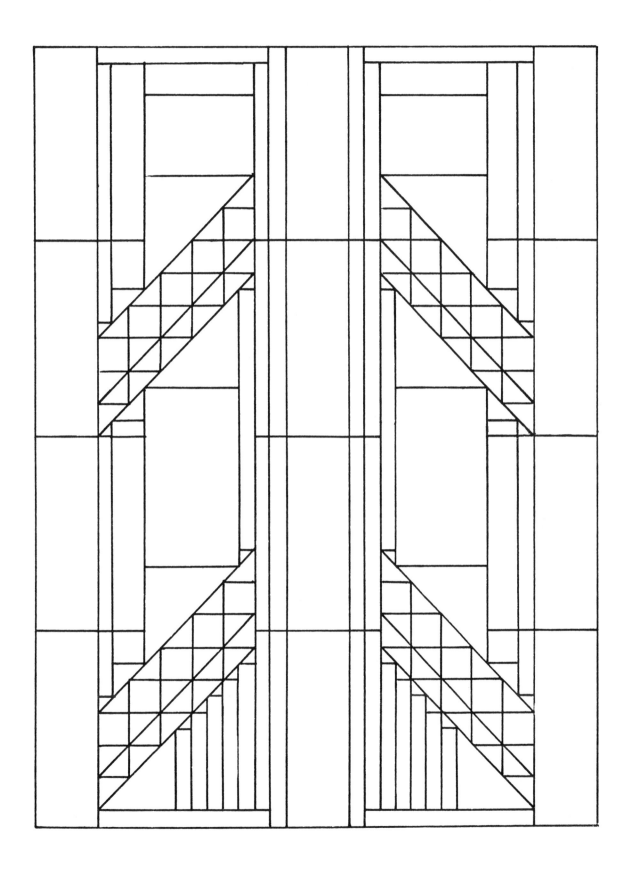

55

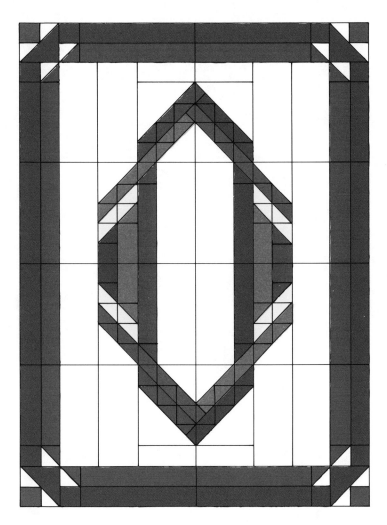

Rose-Colored Glasses

		Template Codes		
Color	Number of templates	Full	Queen	King
Yellow	16	T7	T9	T13
Green	2	T4	T5	T6
	22	T7	T9	T13
	4	R50	R62	R72
Blue	4	S7	S9	S11
	2	T4	T5	T6
	20	T7	T9	T13
Reddish Brown	8	S7	S9	S11
	2	T4	T5	T6
	15	T7	T9	T13
	6	R55	R66	R76
	8	R57	R68	R78

		Template Codes		
Color	Number of templates	Full	Queen	King
Pink	2	S7	S9	S11
	2	T4	T5	T6
	23	T7	T9	T13
	6	R55	R66	R76
	4	R57	R68	R78
	4	R59	R70	R80
White	16	T7	T9	T13
	4	T22	T24	T28
	4	T31	T32	T34
	4	R53	R64	R74
	16	R57	R68	R78
Total	204			

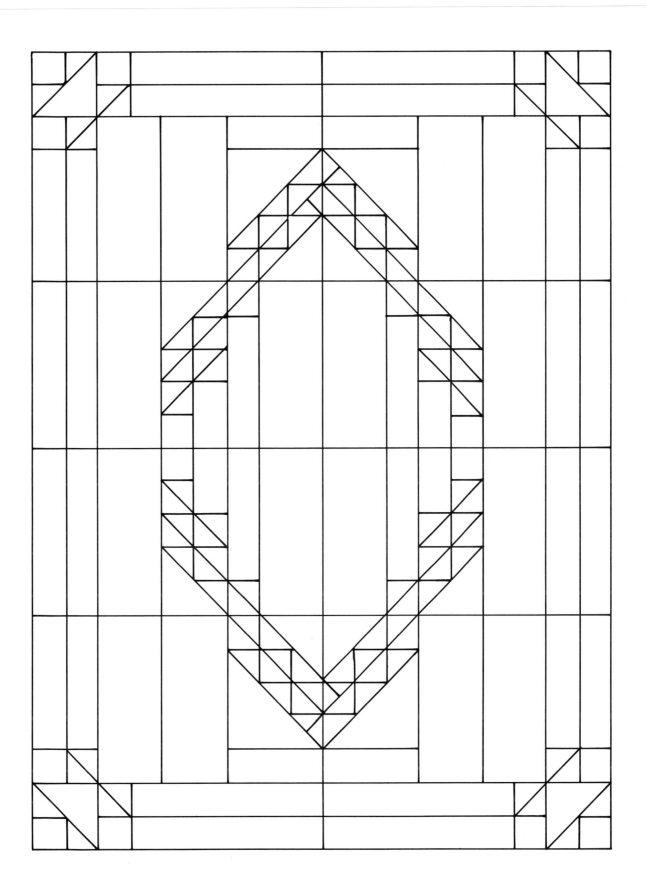

57

Slight Deviations

		Template Codes		
Color	**Number of templates**	**Full**	**Queen**	**King**
White	12	S17	S19	S22
Orange	14	S17	S19	S22
	28	T14	T16	T20
Red	20	S17	S19	S22
	40	T14	T16	T10
Brown	16	S17	S19	S22
	32	T14	T16	T20
Yellow	12	S17	S19	S22
	20	T7	T9	T13
	10	T14	T16	T20
	8	R50	R62	R72
Total	**212**			

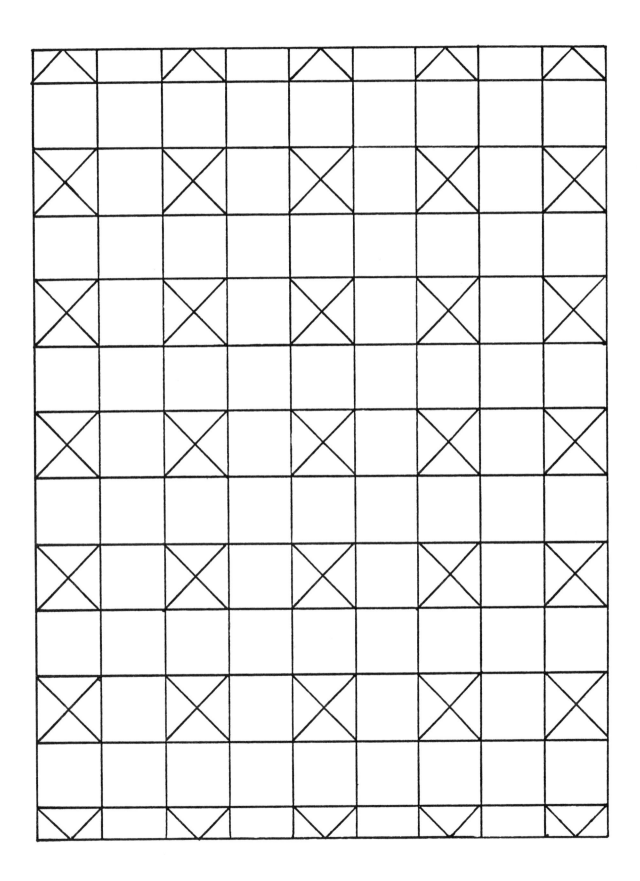

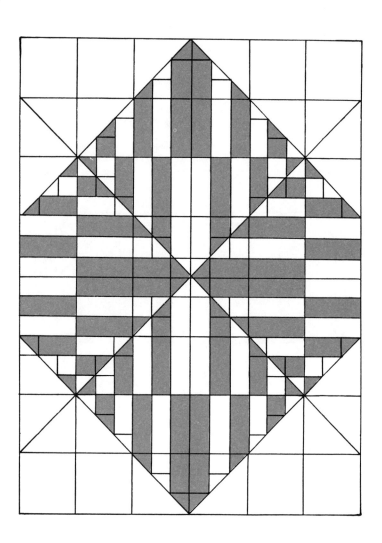

Tiffany

		Template Codes		
Color	Number of templates	Full	Queen	King
Blue	12	S7	S9	S11
	44	T7	T9	T13
	16	R50	R62	R72
	24	R53	R64	R74
White	16	S7	S9	S11
	8	S24	S25	S26
	40	T7	T9	T13
	20	T31	T32	T34
	12	R50	R62	R72
	24	R53	R64	R74
Total	216			

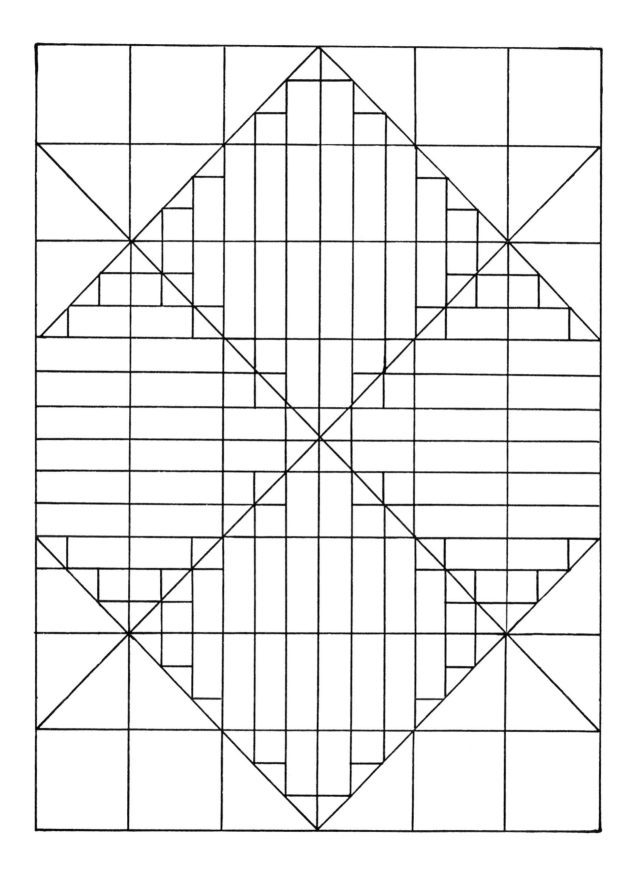

61

Sunday Morning

Color	Number of templates	Template Codes		
		Full	Queen	King
Blue	4	T7	T9	T13
	12	R53	R64	R74
	4	R55	R66	R76
	4	R59	R70	R80
Yellow	6	S7	S9	S11
	8	T7	T9	T13
	4	T22	T24	T28
	4	R50	R62	R72
	8	R53	R64	R74
Green	8	S7	S9	S11
	28	T7	T9	T13
	8	R50	R62	R72
	4	R53	R64	R74
	2	R55	R66	R76

Color	Number of templates	Template Codes		
		Full	Queen	King
	2	R59	R70	R80
Orange	20	S7	S9	S11
	20	T7	T9	T13
	4	R50	R62	R72
	8	R53	R64	R74
	2	R55	R66	R76
	4	R59	R70	R80
White	16	S7	S9	S11
	20	T7	T9	T13
	4	R53	R64	R74
	4	R55	R66	R76
	4	R59	R70	R80
	10	R100	R109	R117
Total	**220**			

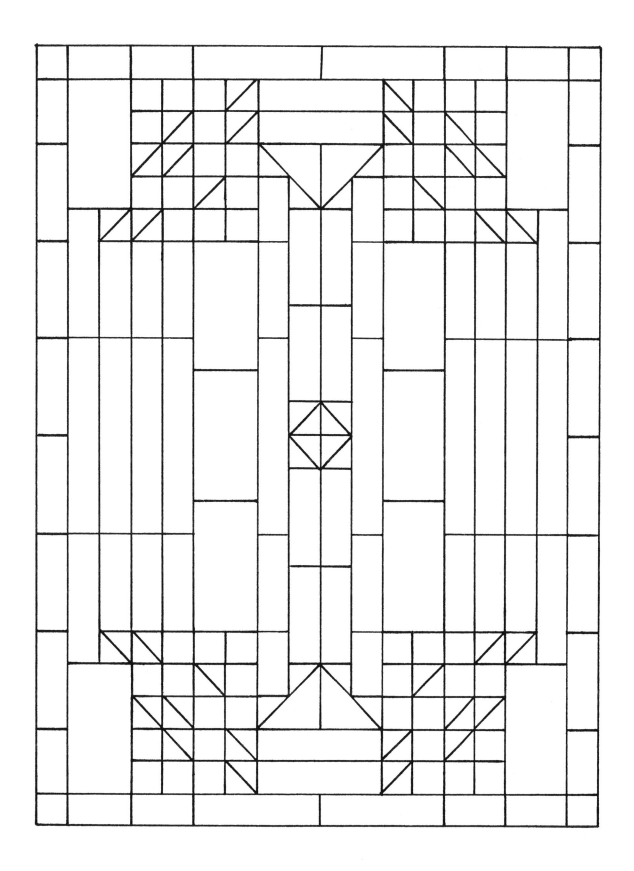

63

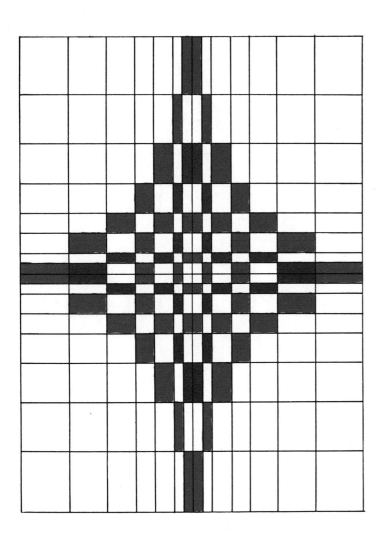

Balancing Act

		Template Codes		
Color	Number of templates	Full	Queen	King
Dark Brown	8	R1	R12	R25
	8	R2	R13	R27
	8	R3	R14	R29
Wine	8	S1	S2	S3
	8	S7	S9	S11
	8	R1	R12	R25
	8	R2	R13	R27
	8	R3	R14	R29
	8	R4	R15	R31
	4	R5	R16	R32
White	8	S1	S2	S3
	8	S7	S9	S11
	4	S13	S15	S17
	4	S17	S19	S22
	4	S21	S28	S25
	16	R1	R12	R25

		Template Codes		
Color	Number of templates	Full	Queen	King
	8	R2	R13	R27
	8	R3	R14	R29
	8	R4	R15	R31
	4	R5	R16	R32
	8	R49	R61	R71
	8	R50	R62	R72
	16	R51	R63	R73
	8	R53	R64	R74
	8	R81	R88	R96
	8	R82	R89	R98
	8	R95	R106	R114
	4	R83	R90	R100
	4	R97	R107	R115
	4	R112	R120	R125
Total	**224**			

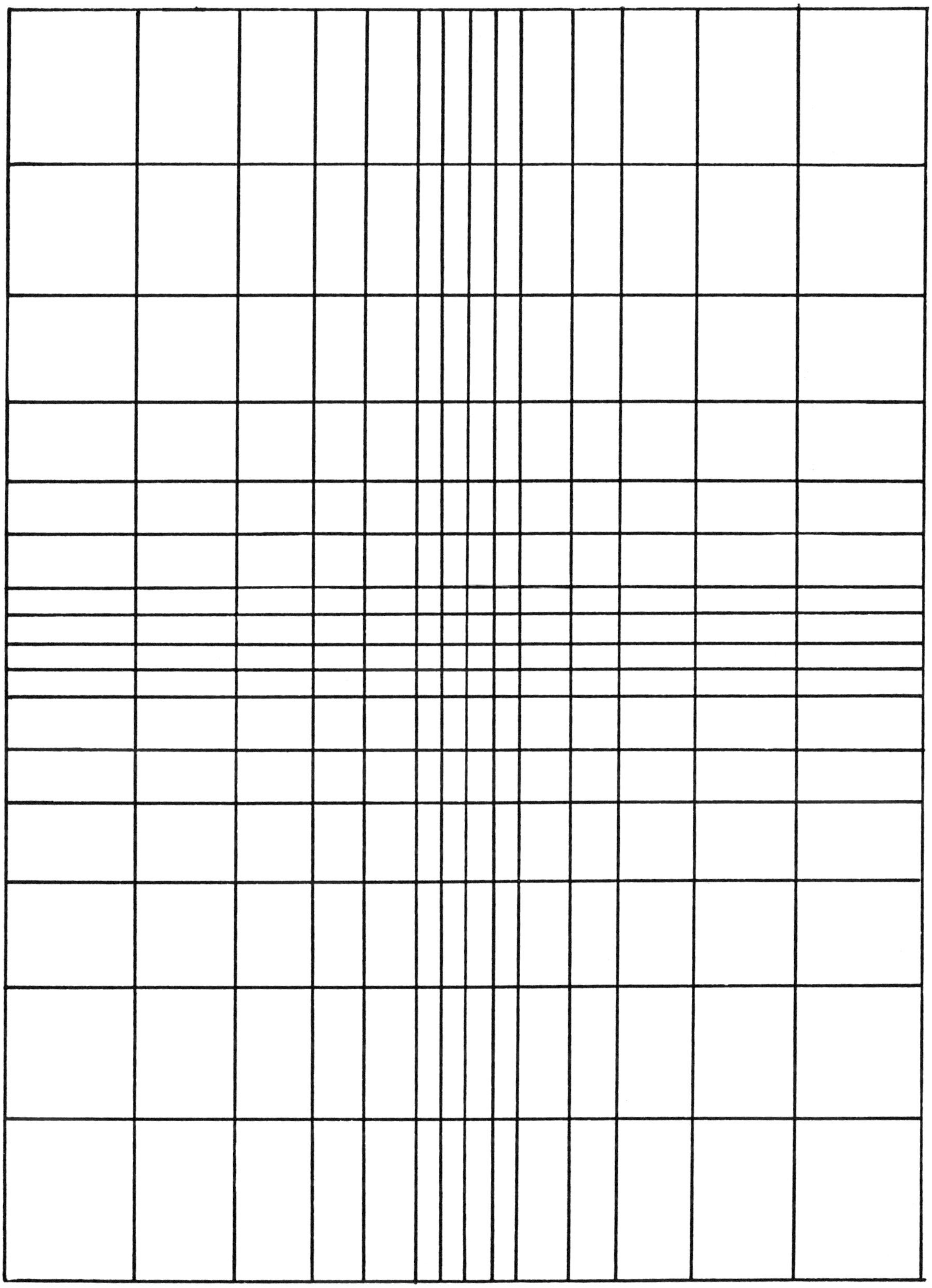

Self-Restraint

		Template Codes		
Color	Number of templates	Full	Queen	King
Yellow	32	T15	T19	T22
	12	T18	T21	T25
	8	R59	R70	R80
Green	24	T15	T19	T22
	16	T18	T21	T25
	8	R11	R23	R38
Red	8	R3	R14	R29
	12	R5	R16	R32
	20	R11	R23	R38
Black	1	S7	S9	S11
	16	T4	T5	T6
	10	R1	R12	R25

		Template Codes		
Color	Number of templates	Full	Queen	King
	8	R3	R14	R29
	4	R5	R16	R32
	10	R11	R23	R38
White	16	T4	T5	T6
	8	T15	T19	T22
	4	T18	T21	T25
	4	R51	R63	R73
	2	R57	R68	R78
	8	R95	R106	R114
	4	R101	R110	R118
Total	235			

67

Tree of Life

Color	Number of templates	Template Codes Full	Queen	King
Light Brown	4	S12	S14	S16
Blue	32	S12	S14	S16
	16	T14	T16	T20
Green	22	S12	S14	S16
	20	T14	T16	T20
Pink	6	S12	S14	S16
	4	S24	S25	S26
	8	T7	T9	T13
	8	T14	T16	T20
Dark Brown	32	S12	S14	S16
	28	T7	T9	T13
	28	T14	T16	T20
	8	R97	R107	R115
Yellow	4	S12	S14	S16
	4	S24	S25	S26
	8	T7	T9	T13
	8	T14	T16	T20
Total	**250**			

69

Checkered Past

Color	Number of templates	Template Codes Full	Queen	King
Green	24	R11	R23	R38
White	8	R83	R90	R100
Burgandy	48	T15	T19	T22
Red	48	S7	S9	S11
	16	R2	R13	R27
Black	48	S7	S9	S11
	16	R2	R13	R27
	8	R11	R23	R38
Yellow	16	T15	T19	T22
	16	T31	T32	T34
	8	R83	R90	R100
Total	**256**			

Anticipation

Color	Number of templates	Template Codes Full	Queen	King
Burgandy	22	T22	T24	T28
	4	R3	R14	R29
	4	R7	R18	R34
	4	R51	R63	R73
Red	8	S7	S9	S11
	22	T22	T24	T28
	8	R3	R14	R29
	4	R7	R18	R34
	2	R50	R62	R72
	4	R59	R70	R80
Orange	20	T7	T9	T13
	18	T15	T19	T22
	2	R2	R13	R27
	4	R7	R18	R34
	4	R49	R61	R71
	1	R53	R64	R74

Color	Number of templates	Template Codes Full	Queen	King
	1	R55	R66	R76
	1	R57	R68	R78
	2	R59	R70	R80
Beige	8	S7	S9	S11
	20	T7	T9	T19
	18	T15	T19	T22
	20	R1	R12	R25
	4	R3	R14	R29
	4	R7	R18	R34
	4	R49	R61	R71
	22	R50	R62	R72
	4	R51	R63	R73
	10	R55	R66	R76
	2	R57	R68	R78
	2	R59	R70	R80
Total	**257**			

Out-of-Bounds

		Template Codes						Template Codes		
Color	Number of templates	Full	Queen	King		Color	Number of templates	Full	Queen	King
Flesh	20	T7	T9	T13			8	R57	R68	R78
	8	R50	R62	R72		Dark Brown	12	S7	S9	S11
Turquoise	40	S7	S9	S11			28	T7	T9	T13
	8	T7	T9	T13			8	R50	R62	R72
	8	T22	T24	T28			8	R53	R64	R74
White	8	S7	S9	S11			4	R57	R68	R78
	8	T7	T9	T13		Light Brown	8	T7	T9	T13
	4	T31	T32	T34			8	T22	T24	T28
	12	R57	R68	R78			4	R50	R62	R72
Pink	12	S7	S9	S11			4	R53	R64	R74
	28	T7	T9	T13			4	R55	R66	R76
	4	R53	R62	R72			4	R57	R68	R78
	4	R55	R66	R76		Total	264			

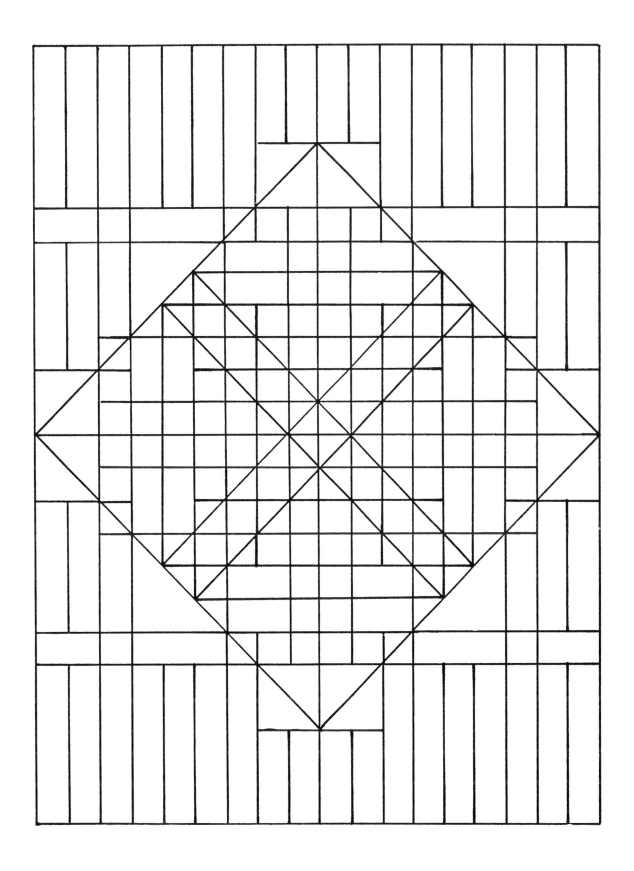

75

Assembly Line

Color	Number of templates	Template Codes Full	Queen	King
Orange	18	R11	R23	R38
Turquoise	96	T42	T43	T44
	24	T39	T40	T41
Brown	72	T42	T43	T44
	48	T39	T40	T41
White	6	R11	R23	R38
	72	T42	T43	T44
	24	T39	T40	T41
Total	**264**			

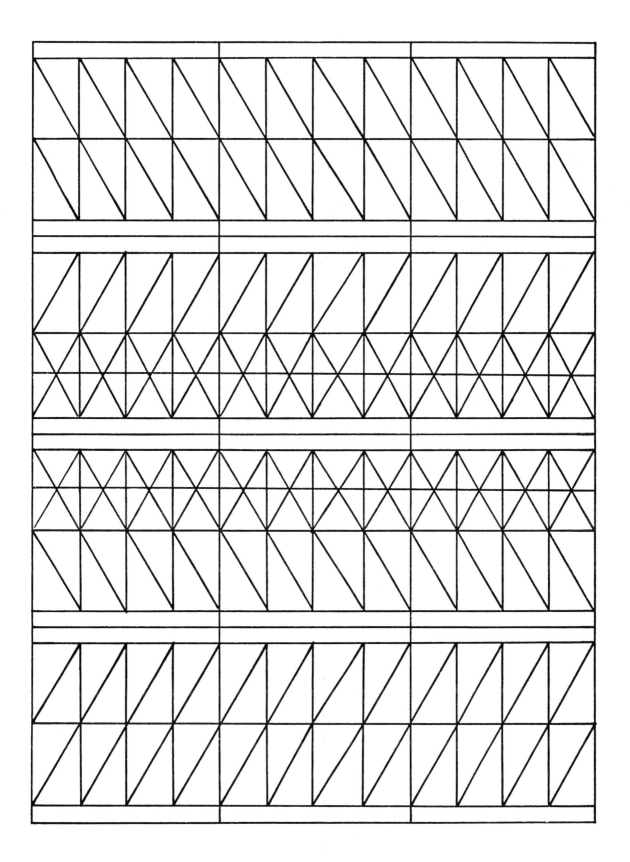

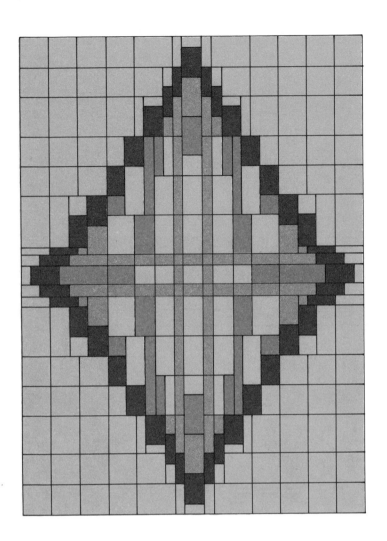

Eye of the Storm

Color	Number of templates	Template Codes Full	Queen	King
Dark Brown	16	R2	R13	R27
	24	R49	R61	R71
Pink	7	S7	S9	S11
	4	R3	R14	R29
	12	R50	R62	R72
	4	R51	R63	R73
	4	R81	R88	R96
Blue	4	S7	S9	S11
	4	R3	R14	R29
	4	R7	R18	R34
	2	R49	R61	R71
	6	R50	R62	R72
	2	R51	R63	R73
Green	8	S1	S2	S3
	16	R1	R12	R25

Color	Number of templates	Template Codes Full	Queen	King
	4	R2	R13	R27
	20	R3	R14	R29
	4	R49	R61	R71
	2	R50	R62	R72
Tan	16	R1	R12	R25
	8	R2	R13	R27
	4	R3	R14	R29
	4	R49	R61	R71
	4	R51	R63	R73
	20	R81	R88	R96
	4	R82	R89	R98
	4	S7	S9	S11
	60	S13	S15	S17
Total	**271**			

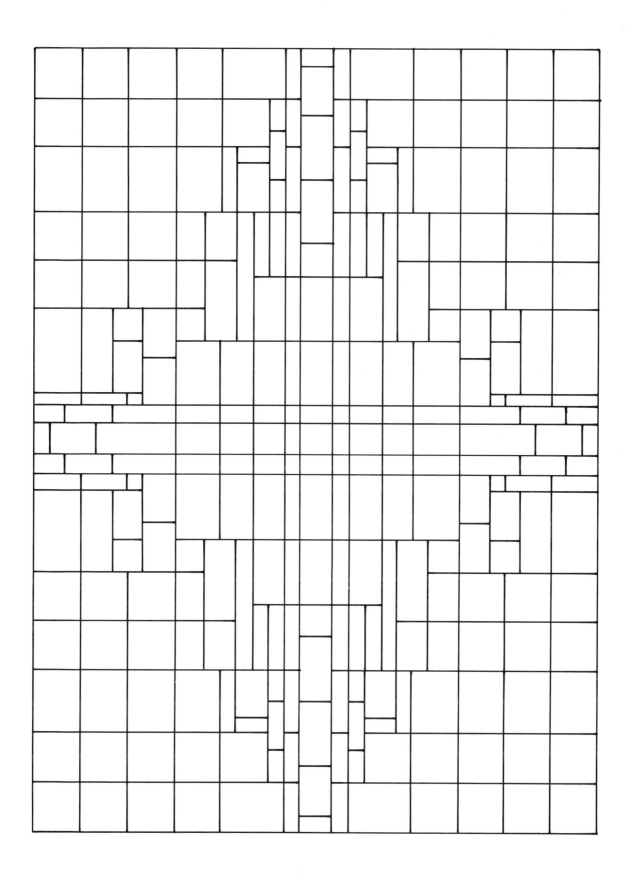

Cat's Whiskers

		Template Codes		
Color	Number of templates	Full	Queen	King
Green	40	T15	T19	T22
Pink	8	S13	S15	S17
	12	T8	T10	T14
	24	T15	T19	T22
Blue	8	S13	S15	S17
	24	T8	T10	T14
	24	T15	T19	T22
Brown	8	S13	S15	S17
	40	T15	T19	T22
	8	R83	R90	R100
White	8	S13	S15	S17
	8	T8	T10	T14
	8	T15	T19	T22
Beige	8	S13	S15	S17
	4	T8	T10	T14
	16	T15	T19	T22
	24	T31	T32	T34
Total	**272**			

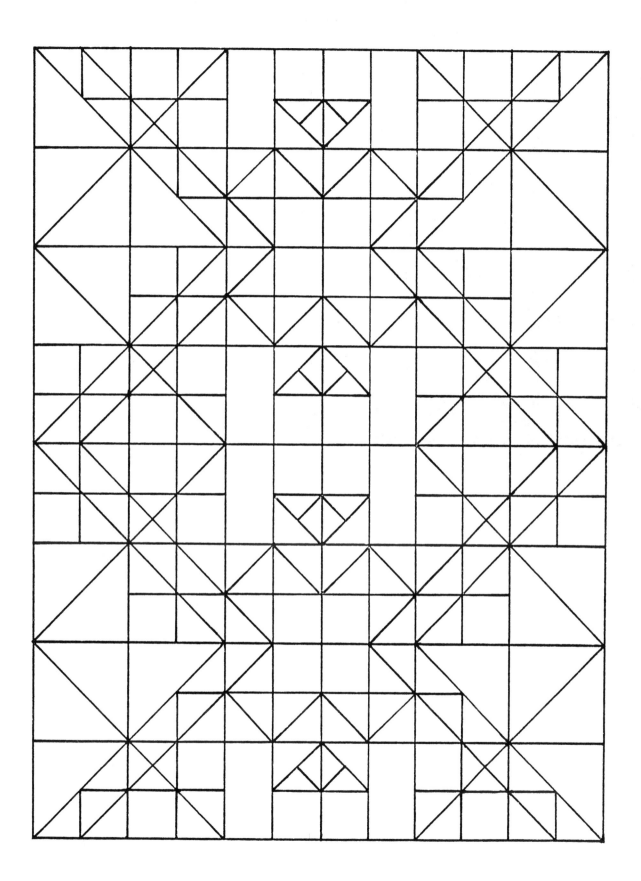

81

Triptych

		Template Codes		
Color	Number of templates	Full	Queen	King
Blue	8	S7	S9	S11
	12	T15	T19	T22
	12	R9	R21	R36
	10	R11	R23	R38
Brown	60	T7	T9	T13
	8	T15	T19	T22
	12	R9	R21	R36
	10	R11	R23	R38
Flesh	8	S1	S2	S3
	4	S13	S15	S17
	60	T7	T9	T13
	16	R53	R64	R74
	16	R85	R92	R103
White	8	S1	S2	S3
	8	S7	S9	S11
	10	S17	S19	S22
	4	T15	T19	T22
	16	R53	R64	R74
	4	R85	R92	R103
Total	**274**			

Mirage

Color	Number of templates	Template Codes		
		Full	Queen	King
Pink	32	T15	T19	T22
Dark Brown	66	T15	T19	T22
Green	50	T15	T19	T22
Red	36	T15	T19	T22
	16	T31	T32	T34
Flesh	2	T15	T19	T22
	64	T15	T19	T22
	14	T31	T32	T34
Total	**280**			

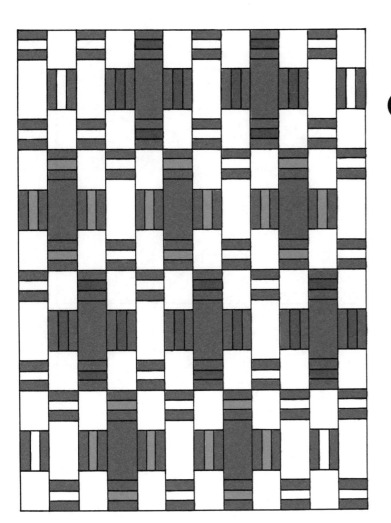

Off Kilter

		Template Codes		
Color	Number of templates	Full	Queen	King
Pink	10	R2	R13	R27
	10	R3	R14	R29
Blue	10	R2	R13	R27
	10	R3	R14	R29
Gray	96	R2	R13	R27
	48	R3	R14	R29
	10	R83	R90	R100
White	28	R2	R13	R27
	4	R3	R14	R29
	48	R81	R88	R96
	14	R83	R90	R100
Total	**288**			

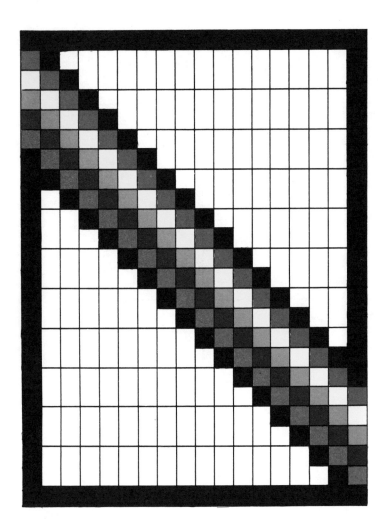

Over the Rainbow

Color	Number of templates	Template Codes Full	Queen	King
Red	18	S7	S9	S11
Yellow	18	S7	S9	S11
Orange	18	S7	S9	S11
Blue	18	S7	S9	S11
Green	18	S7	S9	S11
Black	70	S7	S9	S11
	16	R50	R62	R72
White	16	S7	S9	S11
	112	R50	R62	R72
Total	**304**			

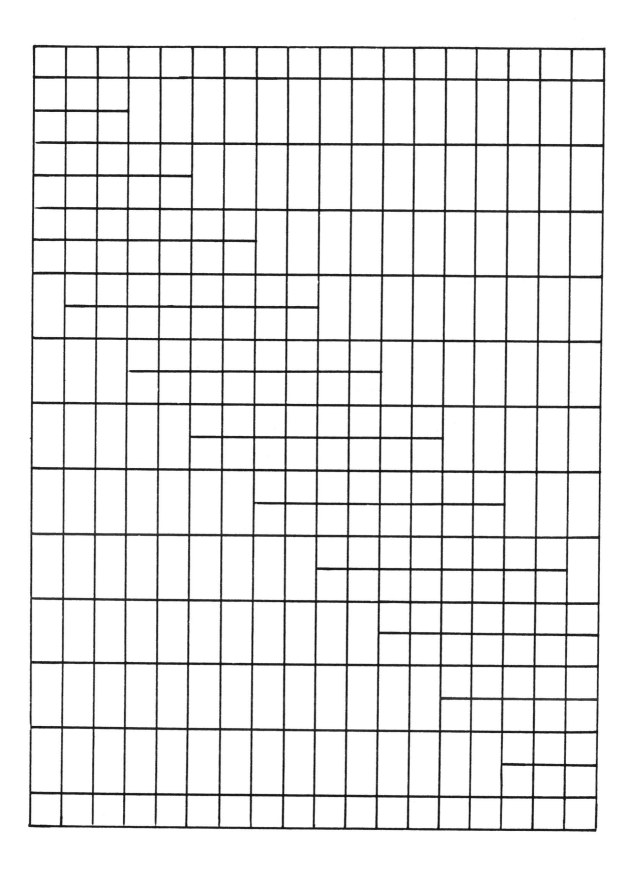

Kaleidoscope

		Template Codes					**Template Codes**		
Color	Number of templates	Full	Queen	King	Color	Number of templates	Full	Queen	King
Burgandy	1	S7	S9	S11		32	R1	R12	R25
	8	S13	S15	S17		24	R2	R13	R27
	4	R49	R61	R71		8	R5	R16	R32
Gold	4	S1	S2	S3		8	R6	R17	R33
	20	R1	R12	R25		12	R49	R61	R71
	32	R2	R13	R27		4	R50	R62	R72
Turquoise	4	S1	S2	S3		4	R51	R63	R73
	32	S7	S9	S11		12	R55	R66	R76
	16	R1	R12	R25		8	R54	R65	R75
	4	R6	R17	R33		2	R56	R67	R77
White	4	S1	S2	S3		4	R85	R92	R103
	52	S7	S9	S11		4	R86	R93	R104
	12	S13	S15	S17	**Total**	**315**			

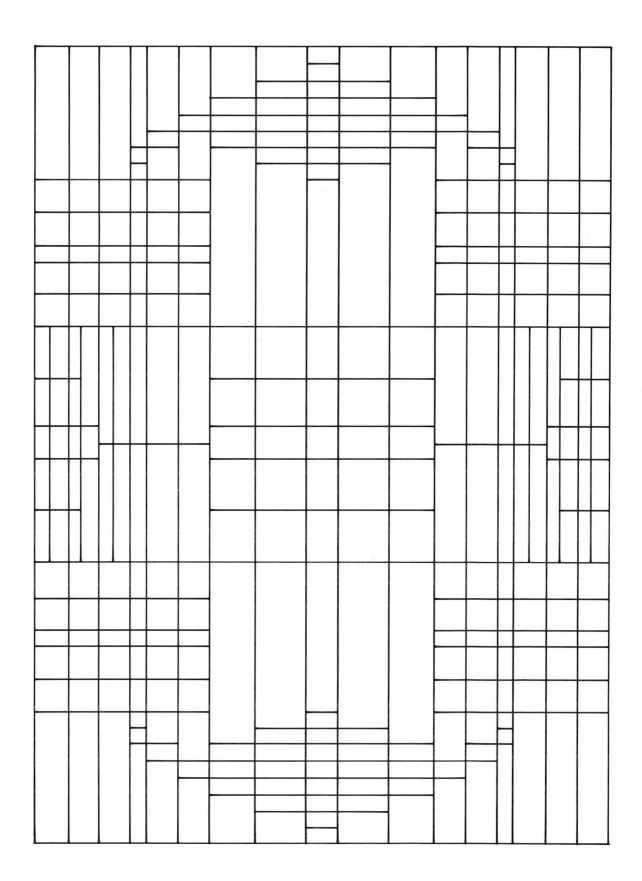

Machismo

Color	Number of templates	Template Codes		
		Full	Queen	King
White	8	S13	S15	S17
	8	T15	T19	T22
	20	T31	T32	T34
Black	16	T7	T9	T13
	24	T15	T19	T22
	4	T22	T24	T28
Green	8	T1	T2	T3
	32	T7	T9	T13
	16	T15	T19	T22
	8	R3	R14	R29
Brown	16	S7	S9	S11
	8	T1	T2	T3
	24	T7	T9	T13
	16	T15	T19	T22

Color	Number of templates	Template Codes		
		Full	Queen	King
	4	T31	T32	T34
	8	R2	R13	R27
Red	4	S1	S2	S3
	28	S7	S9	S11
	4	S13	S15	S17
	36	T7	T9	T13
	4	T22	T24	T28
	4	T31	T32	T34
	8	R1	R12	R25
	8	R49	R61	R71
	8	R83	R90	R100
	4	R97	R107	R115
Total	**328**			

Late Fall Afternoon

		Template Codes		
Color	Number of templates	Full	Queen	King
Orange	108	S7	S9	S11
Beige	24	S7	S9	S11
White	54	S7	S9	S11
Brown	6	S7	S9	S11
	48	R50	R62	R72
Turquoise	60	S7	S9	S11
	6	R50	R62	R72
	24	R53	R64	R74
Total	**330**			

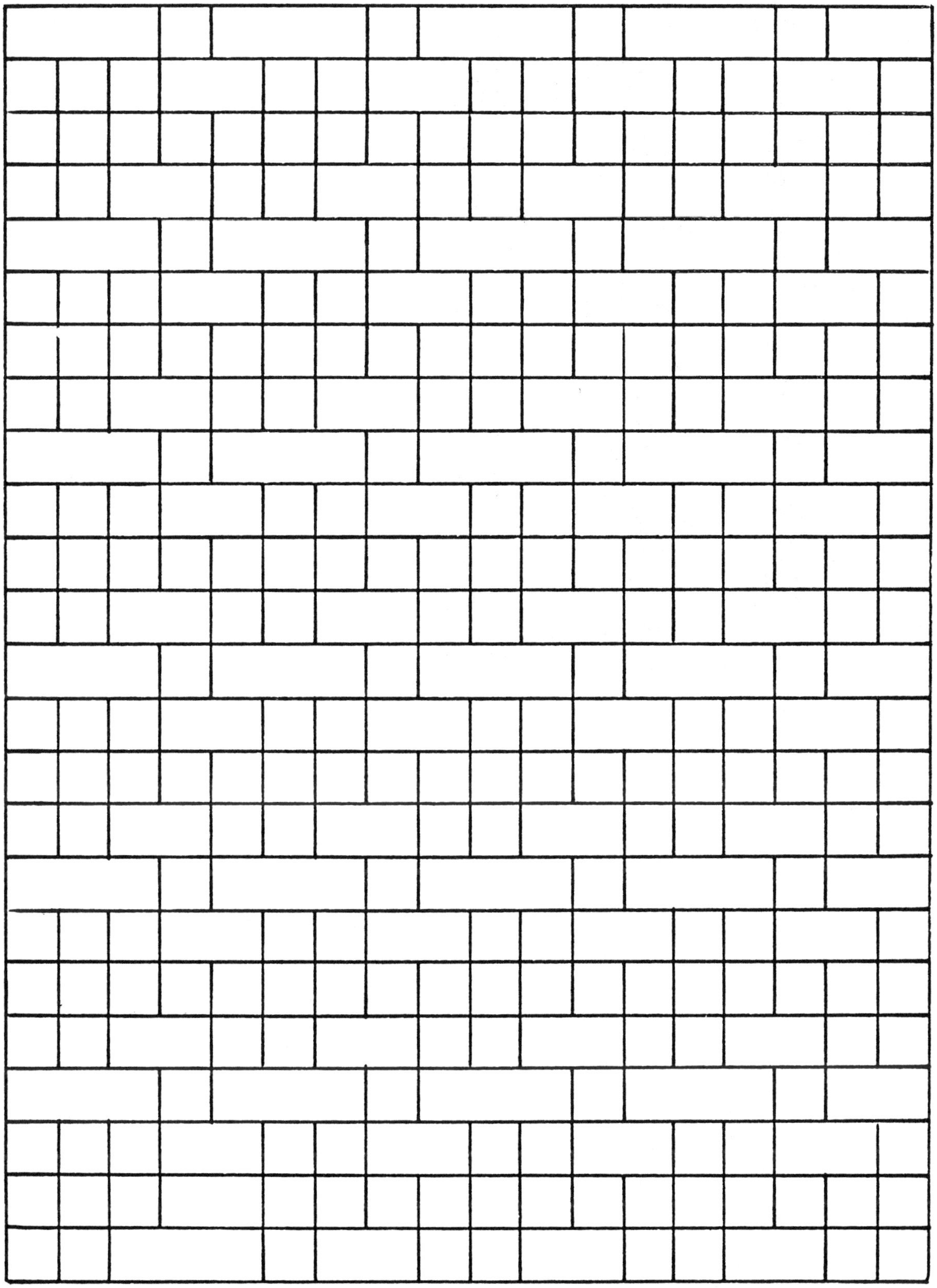

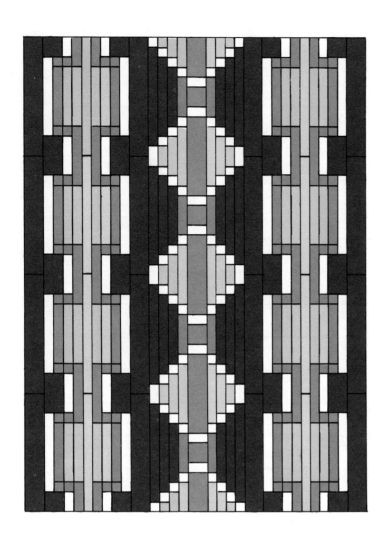

Navajo Necklace

		Template Codes						Template Codes		
Color	Number of templates	Full	Queen	King		Color	Number of templates	Full	Queen	King
White	52	S1	S2	S3			8	R2	R13	R27
	22	R1	R12	R25			8	R3	R14	R29
	12	R3	R14	R29			28	R5	R16	R32
	16	R7	R18	R34			2	R50	R62	R72
Light Blue	4	S1	S2	S3			3	R55	R66	R76
	10	R1	R12	R25		Dark Blue	8	S7	S9	S11
	4	R2	R13	R27			8	R5	R16	R32
	6	R3	R14	R29			8	R7	R18	R34
	38	R5	R16	R32			8	R9	R21	R36
	8	R11	R23	R38			12	R50	R62	R72
Medium Blue	64	S1	S2	S3			16	R59	R70	R80
	4	S7	S9	S11		**Total**	**349**			

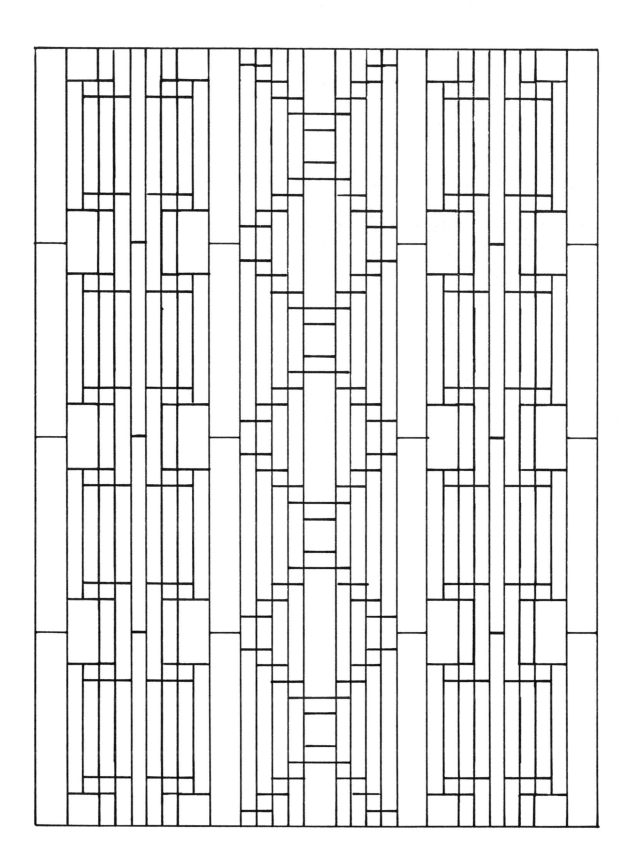

Inner Thoughts

Color	Number of templates	Template Codes		
		Full	Queen	King
Green	24	S7	S9	S11
	88	T7	T9	T13
	32	R1	R12	R25
Orange	24	S7	S9	S11
	20	S17	S19	S22
	40	T7	T9	T13
	24	R50	R62	R72
Red	16	S7	S9	S11
	48	T7	T9	T13
	32	R1	R12	R25
	12	R50	R62	R72
	8	R102	R111	R119
Total	**368**			

99

Bamboo Chimes

Color	Number of templates	Full	Queen	King
Red	48	S1	S2	S3
	2	R1	R12	R25
	4	R10	R22	R37
Blue	72	S1	S2	S3
	4	R1	R12	R25
	4	R3	R14	R29
	8	R7	R18	R34
	4	R8	R20	R35
	4	R9	R21	R36
White	2	R1	R12	R25
	2	R3	R14	R29
	22	R5	R16	R32
	2	R7	R18	R34
	2	R9	R21	R36
	2	R11	R23	R38
Green	20	S1	S2	S3
	12	R1	R12	R25
	8	R2	R13	R27
	4	R3	R14	R29
	8	R7	R18	R34
	16	R51	R63	R73
	4	R50	R62	R72
	4	R53	R64	R74
	8	R56	R67	R77
	12	R59	R70	R80
Yellow	24	S1	S2	S3
	34	R1	R12	R25
	4	R2	R13	R27
	6	R3	R14	R29
	4	R4	R15	R38
	4	R5	R16	R32
	4	R6	R17	R33
	4	R7	R18	R34
	4	R8	R20	R35
	8	R9	R21	R36
	2	R11	R23	R38
Total	**376**			

101

Harlequin

		Template Codes		
Color	Number of templates	Full	Queen	King
Orange	8	T15	T19	T22
Brown	48	T1	T2	T3
Pink	8	S24	S25	S26
	2	T27	T29	T32
	2	R4	R15	R31
	6	R112	R120	R125
Yellow	16	S1	S2	S3
	6	S24	S25	S26
	20	T15	T19	T22
	4	R1	R12	R25
Dark Green	2	T27	T29	T32
	2	R4	R15	R31
Red	20	S1	S2	S3
	48	T1	T2	T3
	6	T15	T19	T22
	2	R1	R12	R25
	6	R5	R16	R32
	4	R50	R62	R72
Medium Green	8	T15	T19	T22
	2	R1	R12	R25

		Template Codes		
Color	Number of templates	Full	Queen	King
	8	R2	R13	R27
	8	R3	R14	R29
	6	R4	R15	R31
	3	R5	R16	R32
Blue	4	S1	S2	S3
	4	T1	T2	T3
	18	T15	T19	T22
	4	R1	R12	R25
	8	R2	R13	R27
	8	R3	R14	R29
	6	R4	R15	R31
	3	R5	R16	R32
White	20	T15	T19	T22
	4	R1	R12	R25
	16	R2	R13	R27
	24	R3	R14	R29
	12	R4	R15	R31
	4	R5	R16	R32
Total	380			

Fallen Leaves

| | | Template Codes | | |
Color	Number of templates	Full	Queen	King
Flesh	40	S5	S27	S7
Light Brown	20	S5	S27	S7
	20	R40	R45	R52
Dark Brown	20	S5	S27	S7
	20	R40	R45	R52
Green	16	S13	S15	S17
	16	T8	T10	T14
	16	T15	T19	T22
Red	44	S13	S15	S17
	48	T8	T10	T14
	40	T15	T19	T22
White	28	S13	S15	S17
	32	T8	T10	T14
	24	T15	T19	T22
Total	**384**			

105

Appalachian Spring

		Template Codes		
Color	Number of templates	Full	Queen	King
Red	24	R1	R12	R25
	2	R7	R18	R34
Dark Green	24	S7	S9	S11
	24	T7	R9	T13
Light Green	20	S7	S9	S11
	24	T7	T9	T13
Dark Blue	12	S7	S9	S11
	48	R49	R61	R71
Light Blue	6	S7	S9	S11
	36	R49	R61	R71
White	56	S7	S9	S11
	24	R1	R12	R25
	4	R7	R18	R34
	2	R11	R23	R38
	80	R49	R61	R71
Total	386			

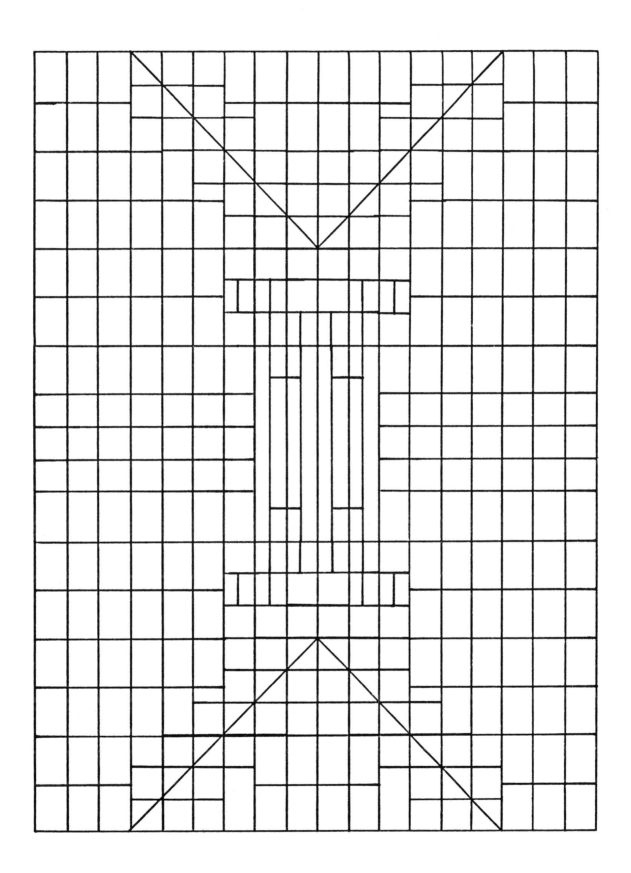

Holding Court

		Template Codes		
Color	Number of templates	Full	Queen	King
Pink	32	T7	T9	T13
	32	R50	R62	R72
Dark Brown	44	T7	T9	T13
	18	R50	R62	R72
Orange	30	S7	S9	S11
	4	T4	T5	T6
	70	T7	T9	T13
	20	R50	R62	R72
Henna	22	S7	S9	S11
	4	T4	T5	T6
	42	T7	T9	T13
	10	R50	R60	R72
Beige	12	S7	S9	S11
	9	S17	S19	S22
	4	S24	S25	S26
	48	T7	T9	T13
Total	**409**			

109

Ticky-Tacky

		Template Codes		
Color	Number of templates	Full	Queen	King
Pink	52	S7	S9	S11
Beige	48	S7	S9	S11
	4	R25	R59	R80
Turquoise	32	S7	S9	S11
	8	T7	T9	T13
	8	R59	R70	R80
Green	192	T7	T9	T13
	4	R55	R66	R76
	4	R57	R68	R78
White	52	S7	S9	S11
	16	T7	T9	T13
	4	T34	T35	T36
Total	424			

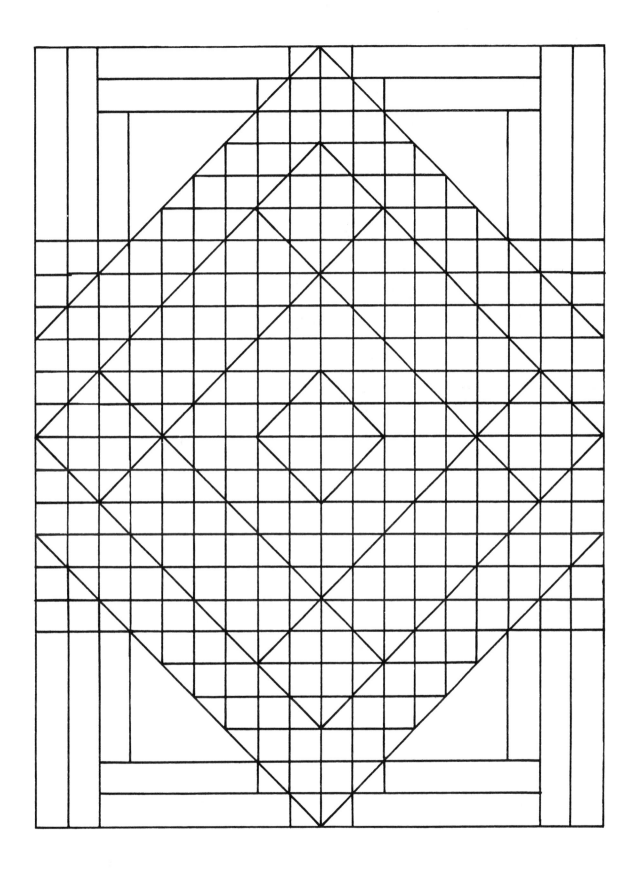

111

Microcosm

Color	Number of templates	Template Codes Full	Queen	King
Dark Green	120	T11	T12	T17
Light Green	96	T11	T12	T17
	18	R49	R61	R71
Medium Green	108	T11	T12	T17
	18	R49	R61	R71
White	60	T11	T12	T17
	60	R49	R61	R71
Total	**480**			

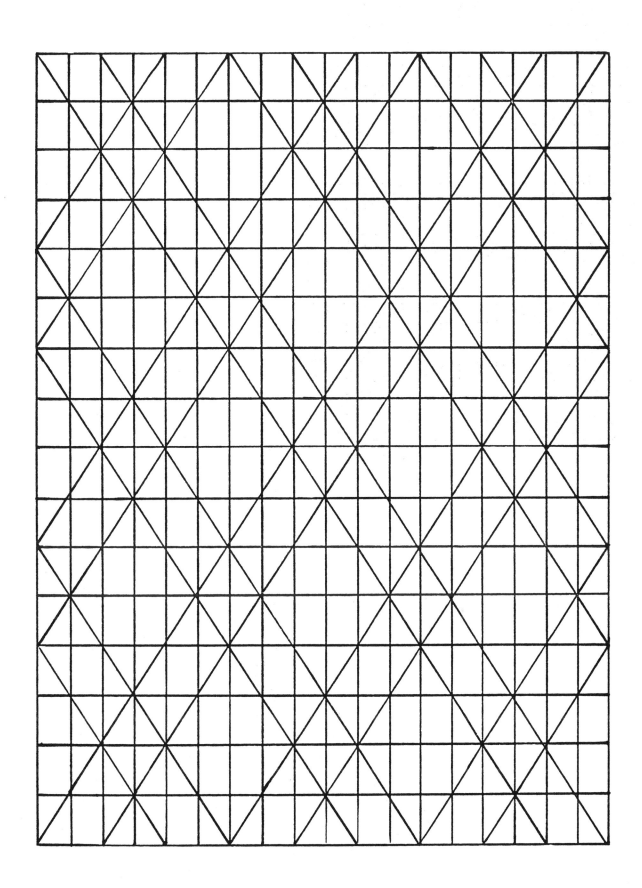

113

Taking Wing

| | | **Template Codes** | | |
Color	Number of templates	Full	Queen	King
Blue	20	S7	S9	S11
	96	T7	T9	T13
Red	24	S7	S9	S11
	78	T7	T9	T13
	8	R50	R62	R72
White	64	T7	T9	T13
	8	R50	R62	R72
	4	R102	R111	R119
Orange	36	S7	S9	S11
	44	T7	T9	T13
	16	R50	R62	R72
Brown	68	S7	S9	S11
	8	S17	S19	S22
	64	T7	T9	T13
Total	**488**			

Egocentric

		Template Codes		
Color	Number of templates	Full	Queen	King
Gold	16	S7	S9	S11
	16	T7	T9	T13
	16	R53	R64	R74
Blue	18	S7	S9	S11
	18	T7	T9	T13
	18	R53	R64	R74
Brown	32	S1	S2	S3
	8	S7	S9	S11
	16	T1	T2	T3
	76	T7	T9	T13
	56	R1	R12	R25
White	48	S1	S2	S3
	10	S7	S9	S11
	16	T1	T2	T3
	78	T7	T9	T13
	40	R1	R12	R25
	8	R7	R18	R34
	16	R11	R23	R38
	16	R53	R64	R74
Total	522			

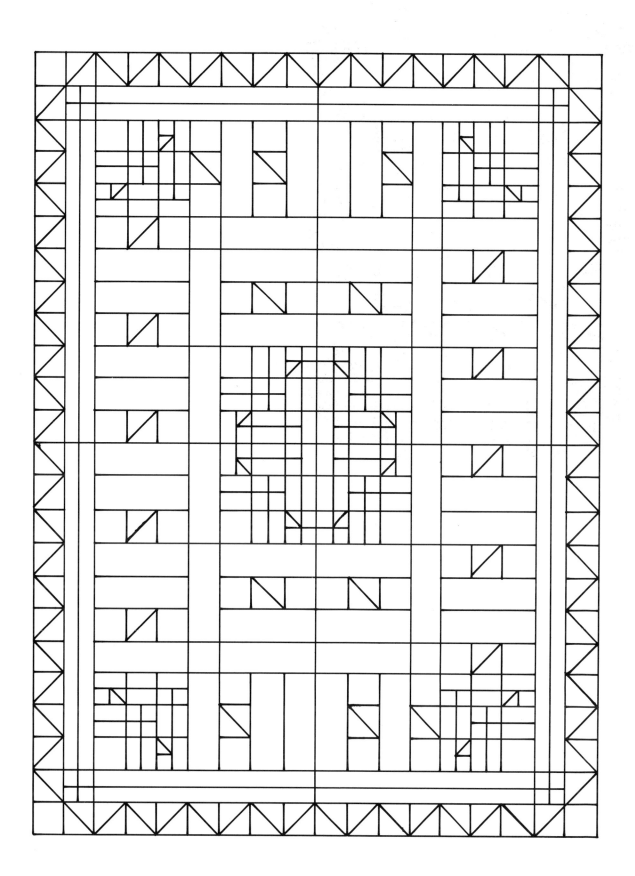

Whirling Dervishes

		Template Codes		
Color	Number of templates	Full	Queen	King
White	52	T7	T9	T13
Red	24	S7	S9	S11
	48	T7	T9	T13
Blue	48	T4	T5	T6
	24	T7	T9	T13
Beige	124	S7	S9	S11
	44	T7	T9	T13
Pink	44	S7	S9	S11
	28	T7	T9	T13
Medium Brown	48	S7	S9	S11
	8	T7	T9	T13
Dark Brown	48	S7	S9	S11
	48	T4	T5	T6
	36	T7	T9	T13
Total	**624**			

119

5
Borders

The border you add to your quilt top will be important in determining the overall look of your quilt. You can either echo the design of the quilt top or choose an entirely new design. The borders in this section give you the choice of either.

Each border design repeats within a certain number of inches. Since the standard mattress sizes vary, we have designed a number of borders which, when used with one of the standard mattress tops, will give full repeats along all four sides. So in order to have complete repeats all around your quilt, refer to the chart below to see which of the border designs will fit your quilt.

Quilt size	Number of inches in repeat	Number of repeats on top and bottom	Number of repeats on each side
Full	9″	6	3
	18″	3	4
Queen	10″	6	8
	20″	3	4
King	12″	6	8
	24″	3	4

See the following illustration for the placement of the borders and the repeats along the sides, top and bottom.

The top and right side of the illustration show the number of repeats for the 9″, 10″ and 12″ repeats; the bottom and left side show the number of repeats for the 18″, 20″ and 24″ repeats.

There are many other ways you could use the designs in this section besides borders on quilts:

Corners: Instead of leaving the corners of the quilt plain (not pieced), you could use a portion of the border for the corner. This works especially well when the design is contained within a square shape and doesn't depend on other pieces to create the full effect of the design.

Crib quilts: Crib quilts generally measure 36″ × 45″ although the size of cribs can vary—especially if the mother-to-be buys an antique crib! So any of the 9-inch border repeats could be used to make a crib quilt by simply making two borders using 5 repeats of the design and sewing them together to make the entire quilt top.

Pillows: Any of the designs, but especially the more intricate ones can be made into beautiful patchwork pillows.

And these are just a few ideas. Think about wall hangings, clothing, table cloths—in fact, anywhere where a good design will add that extra creative touch to you, your apartment or home, or to your gifts for those you love.

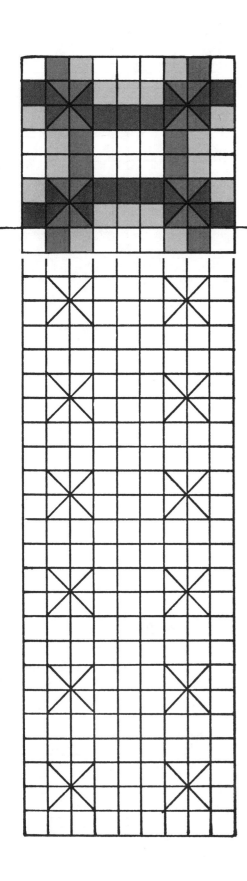

Design No. 1

Border Size 18 inches in width
Pattern Repeat 24 inches
Quilt Size King
Number of Repeats for entire Quilt 14
Frame Measurements:
 Side Panels: 4 inches by 140 inches
 Top and Bottom Panels: 4 inches by 116 inches
Corner Measurements: 18 inches square

Color	Number of templates in repeat	Number of templates in total border	Template code
Yellow	18	252	S7
White	20	280	S7
Orange	8	112	S7
	16	224	T7
Brown	10	140	S7
	16	224	T7
Total	**88**	**1,232**	

Design No. 2

Border Size 18 inches in width
Pattern Repeat 12 inches
Quilt Size King
Number of Repeats for entire Quilt 28
Frame Measurements:
   Side Panels: 4 inches by 140 inches
    Top and Bottom Panels: 4 inches by 116 inches
Corner Measurements: 18 inches square

Color	Number of templates in repeat	Number of templates in total border	Template code
Yellow	6	168	T7
Green	4	112	T22
Red	8	224	T7
Blue	2	56	S7
	4	112	T7
White	8	224	S7
	16	448	T3
Total	**48**	**1,344**	

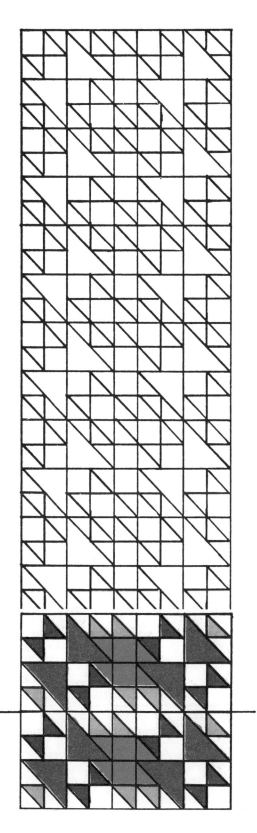

123

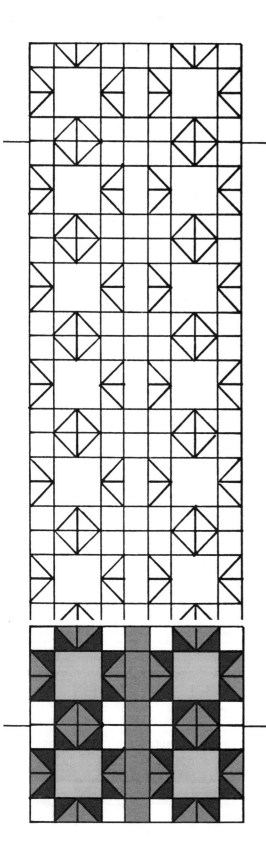

Design No. 3

Border Size 18 inches in width
Pattern Repeat 12 inches
Quilt Size King
Number of Repeats for entire Quilt 28
Frame Measurements:
  Side Panels: 4 inches by 140 inches
    Top and Bottom Panels: 4 inches by 116 inches
Corner Measurements: 18 inches square

Color	Number of templates in repeat	Number of templates in total border	Template code
Beige	4	112	S11
Brown	16	448	T7
White	8	224	S7
Green	2	56	S7
	16	448	T7
	1	28	R50
Total	**46**	**1,288**	

Design No. 4

Border Size   18   inches in width
Pattern Repeat   12   inches
Quilt Size   King
Number of Repeats for entire Quilt   28
Frame Measurements:
   Side Panels: 4   inches by   140   inches
    Top and Bottom Panels: 4   inches by   116   inches
Corner Measurements: 18   inches square

Color	Number of templates in repeat	Number of templates in total border	Template code
Blue	4	112	S17
Yellow	6	168	T7
Red	4	112	T7
	4	112	R50
White	6	168	S7
	2	56	T7
Total	**26**	**728**	

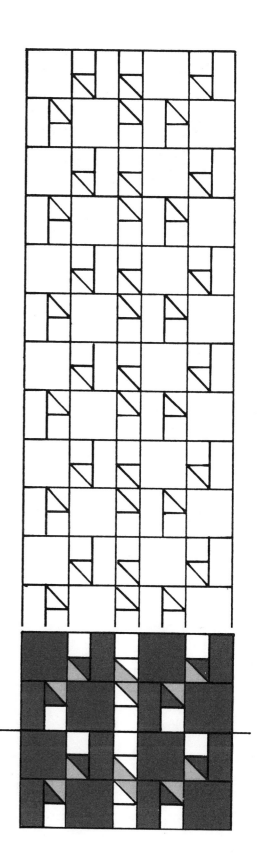

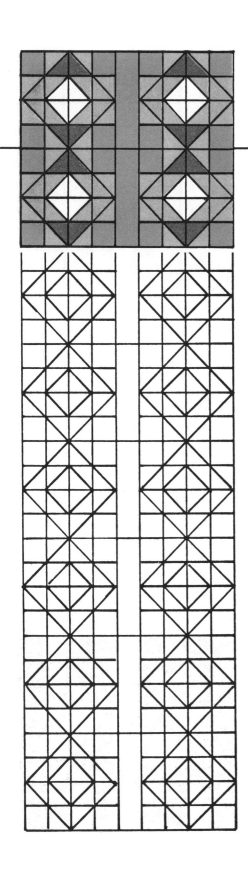

Design No. 5

Border Size 18 inches in width
Pattern Repeat 12 inches
Quilt Size King
Number of Repeats for entire Quilt 28
Frame Measurements:
   Side Panels: 4 inches by 140 inches
    Top and Bottom Panels: 4 inches by 116 inches
Corner Measurements: 18 inches square

Color	Number of templates in repeat	Number of templates in total border	Template code
Light Green	8	224	T7
Dark Green	8	224	T7
Yellow	24	672	T7
White	8	224	T7
Gray	8	224	S7
	2	56	R55
Total	**58**	**1,624**	

Design No. 6

Border Size 18 inches in width
Pattern Repeat 12 inches
Quilt Size King
Number of Repeats for entire Quilt 28
Frame Measurements:
   Side Panels: 4 inches by 140 inches
    Top and Bottom Panels: 4 inches by 116 inches
Corner Measurements: 18 inches square

Color	Number of templates in repeat	Number of templates in total border	Template code
White	8	224	T14
Red	4	112	T14
	4	112	T22
Brown	4	112	T14
	4	112	T22
Total	**24**	**672**	

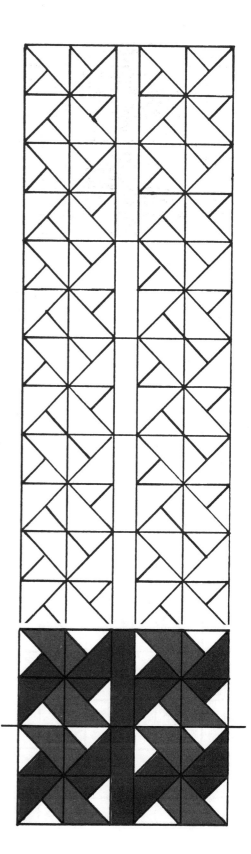

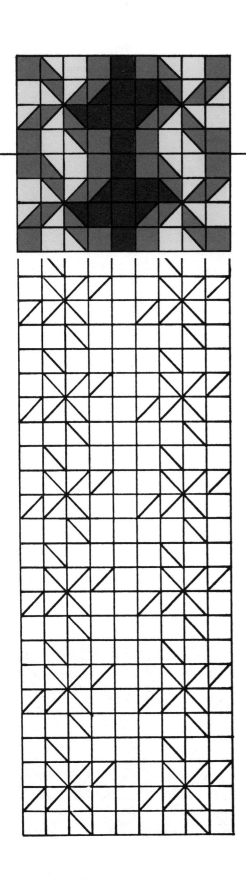

Design No. 7

Border Size 18 inches in width
Pattern Repeat 12 inches
Quilt Size King
Number of Repeats for entire Quilt 28
Frame Measurements:
  Side Panels: 4 inches by 140 inches
  Top and Bottom Panels: 4 inches by 116 inches
Corner Measurements: 18 inches square

Color	Number of templates in repeat	Number of templates in total border	Template code
Dark Blue	6	168	S7
	4	112	T7
Medium Blue	8	224	S7
	16	448	T7
Light Blue	6	168	S7
	12	336	T7
Total	**52**	**1,456**	

Design No. 8

Border Size 18 inches in width
Pattern Repeat 12 inches
Quilt Size King
Number of Repeats for entire Quilt 28
Frame Measurements:
    Side Panels: 4 inches by 140 inches
    Top and Bottom Panels: 4 inches by 116 inches
Corner Measurements: 18 inches square

Color	Number of templates in repeat	Number of templates in total border	Template code
Salmon	5	140	S7
	16	448	T7
Green	5	140	S7
	16	448	T7
White	2	56	S7
	16	448	T7
Total	**60**	**1,680**	

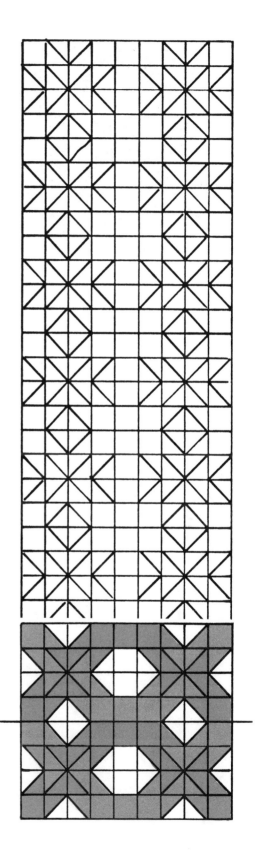

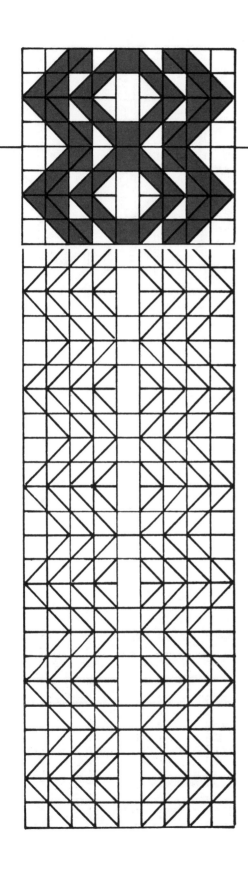

Design No. 9

Border Size   18   inches in width
Pattern Repeat   12   inches
Quilt Size   King
Number of Repeats for entire Quilt   28
Frame Measurements:
   Side Panels: 4   inches by   140   inches
    Top and Bottom Panels: 4   inches by   116   inches
Corner Measurements: 18   inches square

Color	Number of templates in repeat	Number of templates in total border	Template code
Red	8	224	T7
Blue	2	56	S7
	28	784	T7
White	4	112	S7
	20	560	T7
	1	28	R50
Total	**63**	**1,764**	

Design No. 10

Border Size   18   inches in width
Pattern Repeat   12   inches
Quilt Size   King
Number of Repeats for entire Quilt   28
Frame Measurements:
  Side Panels: 4   inches by   140   inches
   Top and Bottom Panels: 4   inches by   116   inches
Corner Measurements: 18   inches square

Color	Number of templates in repeat	Number of templates in total border	Template code
Yellow	8	224	S7
Green	2	56	S7
	1	28	R53
Red	2	56	S7
	1	28	R53
Brown	2	56	S7
	4	112	R55
Total	**20**	**560**	

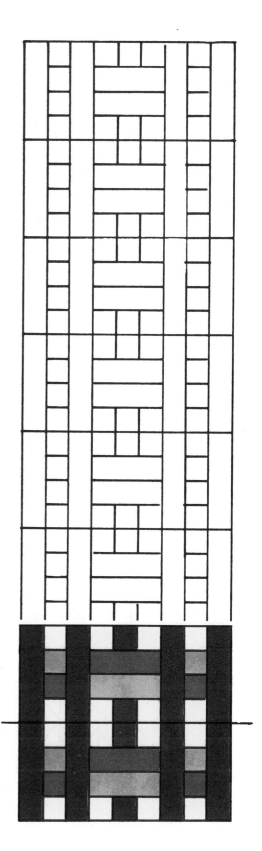

131

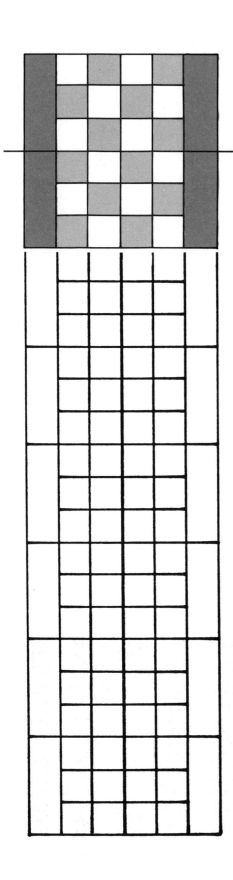

Design No. 11

Border Size   18   inches in width
Pattern Repeat   9   inches
Quilt Size   Full
Number of Repeats for entire Quilt   28
Frame Measurements:
   Side Panels: 4   inches by   116   inches
   Top and Bottom Panels: 4   inches by   98   inches
Corner Measurements: 18   inches square

Color	Number of templates in repeat	Number of templates in total border	Template code
Yellow	6	168	S7
White	6	168	S7
Blue	2	56	R53
Total	**14**	**392**	

Design No. 12

Border Size 18 inches in width
Pattern Repeat 18 inches
Quilt Size Full
Number of Repeats for entire Quilt 14
Frame Measurements:
  Side Panels: 4 inches by 116 inches
  Top and Bottom Panels: 4 inches by 98 inches
Corner Measurements: 18 inches square

Color	Number of templates in repeat	Number of templates in total border	Template code
Blue	12	168	R1
Henna	12	168	R1
Green	12	168	R1
White	21	294	R1
Orange	9	126	R1
	3	42	S7
Total	**69**	**966**	

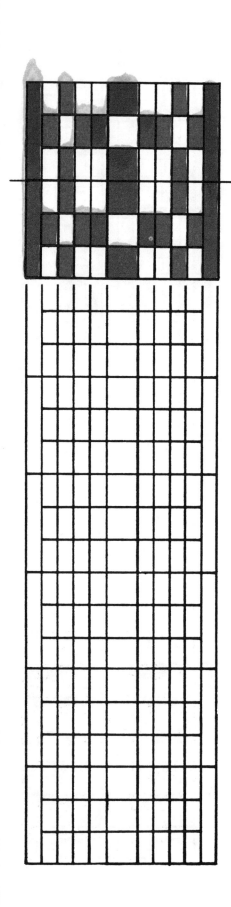

Design No. 13

Border Size 18 inches in width
Pattern Repeat 9 inches
Quilt Size Full
Number of Repeats for entire Quilt 28
Frame Measurements:
  Side Panels: 4 inches by 116 inches
  Top and Bottom Panels: 4 inches by 98 inches
Corner Measurements: 18 inches square

Color	Number of templates in repeat	Number of templates in total border	Template code
White	14	392	R1
Red	8	224	R1
Henna	2	56	R1
	2	56	S7
	2	56	R5
Total	**28**	**784**	

Design No. 14

Border Size 18 inches in width
Pattern Repeat 9 inches
Quilt Size Full
Number of Repeats for entire Quilt 28
Frame Measurements:
    Side Panels: 4 inches by 116 inches
    Top and Bottom Panels: 4 inches by 98 inches
Corner Measurements: 18 inches square

Color	Number of templates in repeat	Number of templates in total border	Template code
Green	1	28	S7
Orange	4	112	S7
Brown	1	28	S7
	2	56	R50
Blue	1	28	S7
	2	56	R50
	2	56	R5
Total	**13**	**364**	

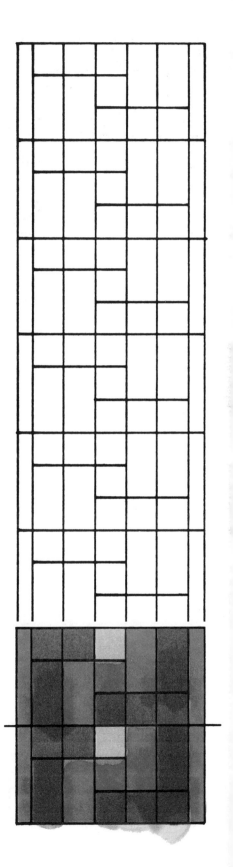

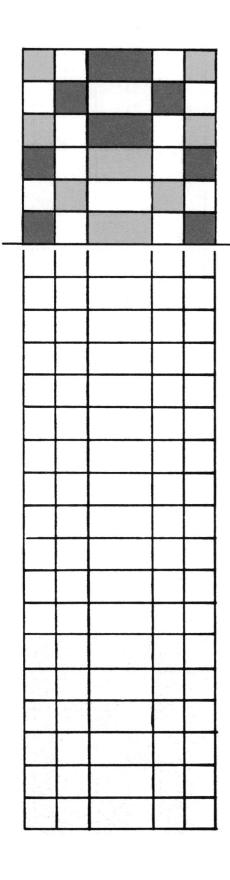

Design No. 15

Border Size   18   inches in width
Pattern Repeat   18   inches
Quilt Size   Full
Number of Repeats for entire Quilt   14
Frame Measurements:
  Side Panels: 4   inches by   116   inches
  Top and Bottom Panels: 4   inches by   98   inches
Corner Measurements: 18   inches square

Color	Number of templates in repeat	Number of templates in total border	Template code
Yellow	6	84	S7
	2	28	R50
Brown	6	84	S7
	2	28	R50
White	12	168	S7
	2	28	R50
Total	**30**	**420**	

Design No. 16

Border Size   18   inches in width
Pattern Repeat   9   inches
Quilt Size   Full
Number of Repeats for entire Quilt   28
Frame Measurements:
  Side Panels: 4   inches by   116   inches
  Top and Bottom Panels: 4   inches by   98   inches
Corner Measurements: 18   inches square

Color	Number of templates in repeat	Number of templates in total border	Template code
Green	2	56	R5
Blue	2	56	R5
White	12	336	T7
Orange	12	336	T7
Total	**28**	**784**	

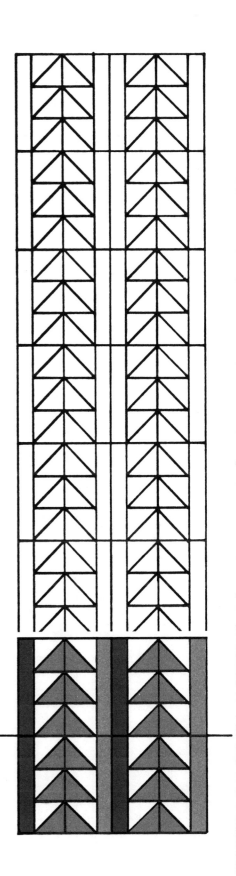

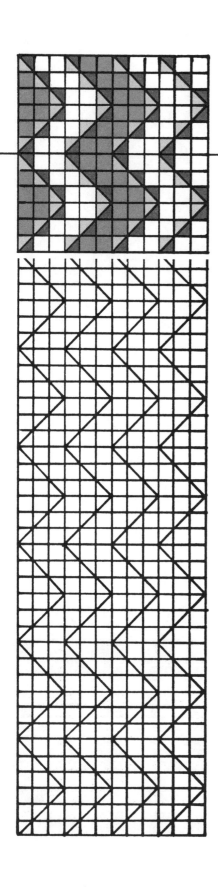

Design No. 17

Border Size 18 inches in width
Pattern Repeat 9 inches
Quilt Size Full
Number of Repeats for entire Quilt 28
Frame Measurements:
   Side Panels: 4 inches by 116 inches
    Top and Bottom Panels: 4 inches by 98 inches
Corner Measurements: 18 inches square

Color	Number of templates in repeat	Number of templates in total border	Template code
White	30	840	S1
Light Green	24	672	T1
Dark Green	24	672	T1
Salmon	18	504	S1
Total	**96**	**2,688**	

Design No. 18

Border Size 18 inches in width
Pattern Repeat 18 inches
Quilt Size Full
Number of Repeats for entire Quilt 14
Frame Measurements:
   Side Panels: 4 inches by 116 inches
    Top and Bottom Panels: 4 inches by 98 inches
Corner Measurements: 18 inches square

Color	Number of templates in repeat	Number of templates in total border	Template code
Pink	21	294	R1
Gray	21	294	R1
White	21	294	S7
Total	**63**	**882**	

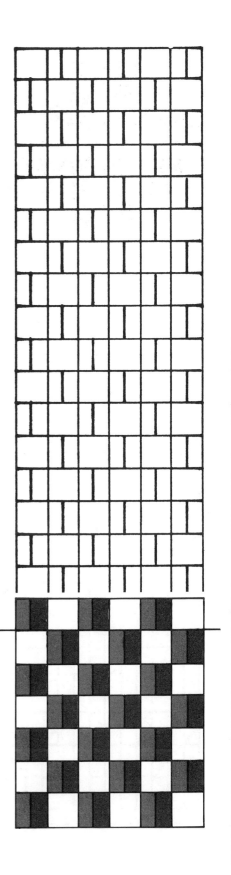

Design No. 19

Border Size   18   inches in width
Pattern Repeat   18   inches
Quilt Size   Full
Number of Repeats for entire Quilt   14
Frame Measurements:
   Side Panels: 4   inches by   116   inches
    Top and Bottom Panels: 4   inches by   98   inches
Corner Measurements: 18   inches square

Color	Number of templates in repeat	Number of templates in total border	Template code
Turquoise	4	56	S1
	4	56	R1
Green	4	56	R4
	4	56	R5
Brown	4	56	R2
	4	56	R3
White	4	56	S1
	4	56	R1
	4	56	R2
	4	56	R3
	4	56	R4
Total	**44**	**616**	

Design No. 20

Border Size 18 inches in width
Pattern Repeat 18 inches
Quilt Size   Full
Number of Repeats for entire Quilt 14
Frame Measurements:
  Side Panels: 4 inches by 116 inches
   Top and Bottom Panels: 4 inches by 98 inches
Corner Measurements: 18 inches square

Color	Number of templates in repeat	Number of templates in total border	Template code
White	8	112	R1
	4	56	R49
	2	28	R81
Blue	8	112	S1
	4	56	R2
	10	140	R49
Total	**36**	**504**	

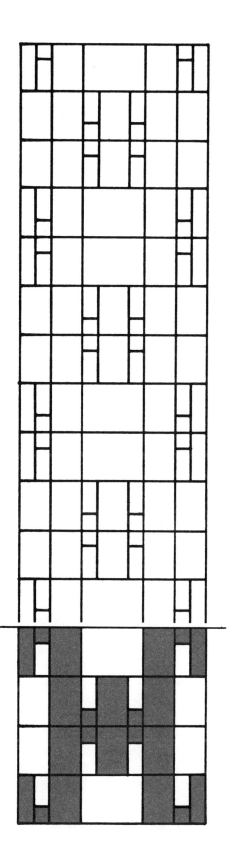

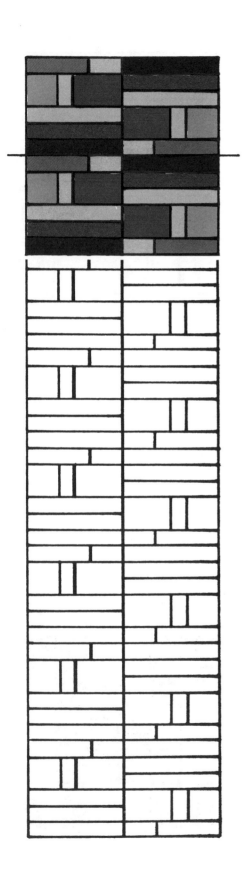

Design No. 21

Border Size 18 inches in width
Pattern Repeat 9 inches
Quilt Size Full
Number of Repeats for entire Quilt 28
Frame Measurements:
  Side Panels: 4 inches by 116 inches
  Top and Bottom Panels: 4 inches by 98 inches
Corner Measurements: 18 inches square

Color	Number of templates in repeat	Number of templates in total border	Template code
Black	2	56	R5
Henna	2	56	R5
Yellow	2	56	R1
Light Pink	2	56	S7
Dark Pink	2	56	R49
Purple	2	56	R3
Beige	2	56	R1
	2	56	R5
Total	**16**	**448**	

Design No. 22

Border Size 18 inches in width
Pattern Repeat 9 inches
Quilt Size Full
Number of Repeats for entire Quilt 28
Frame Measurements:
  Side Panels: 4 inches by 116 inches
  Top and Bottom Panels: 4 inches by 98 inches
Corner Measurements: 18 inches square

Color	Number of templates in repeat	Number of templates in total border	Template code
Green	6	168	R1
Red	4	112	S1
	2	56	R49
Yellow	1	28	S7
	2	56	R1
	2	56	R5
White	4	112	S1
	4	112	S7
	2	56	R1
Total	**27**	**756**	

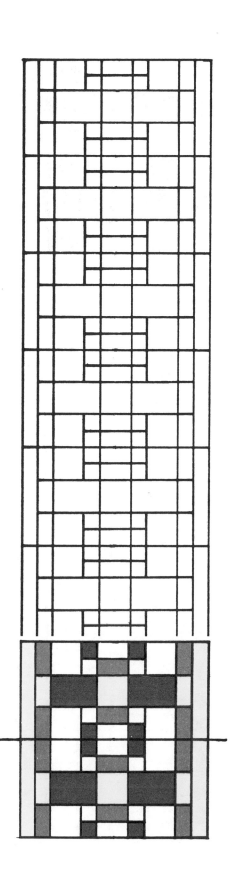

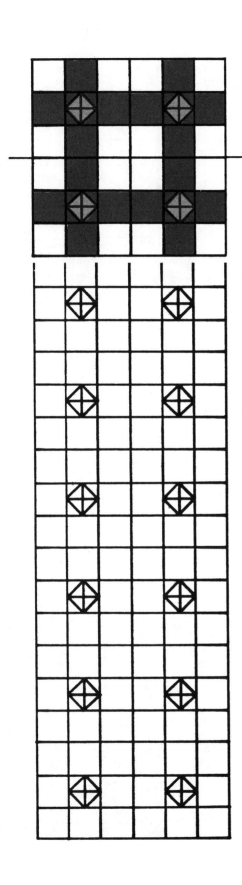

Design No. 23

Border Size   18   inches in width
Pattern Repeat   9   inches
Quilt Size   Full
Number of Repeats for entire Quilt   28
Frame Measurements:
  Side Panels: 4 inches by 116 inches
  Top and Bottom Panels: 4 inches by 98 inches
Corner Measurements: 18 inches square

Color	Number of templates in repeat	Number of templates in total border	Template code
White	8	224	S7
Green	8	224	T1
Blue	8	224	S7
	8	224	T1
Total	**32**	**896**	

Design No. 24

Border Size 18 inches in width
Pattern Repeat 9 inches
Quilt Size Full
Number of Repeats for entire Quilt 28
Frame Measurements:
   Side Panels: 4 inches by 116 inches
   Top and Bottom Panels: 4 inches by 98 inches
Corner Measurements: 18 inches square

Color	Number of templates in repeat	Number of templates in total border	Template code
White	6	168	S1
	2	56	R2
	2	56	R3
Orange	6	168	S1
	2	56	R2
	2	56	R3
	2	56	R81
Total	**22**	**616**	

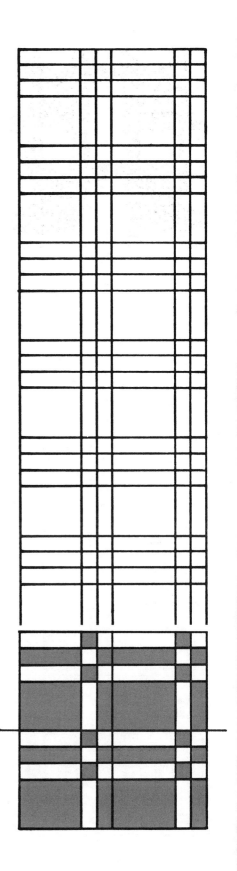

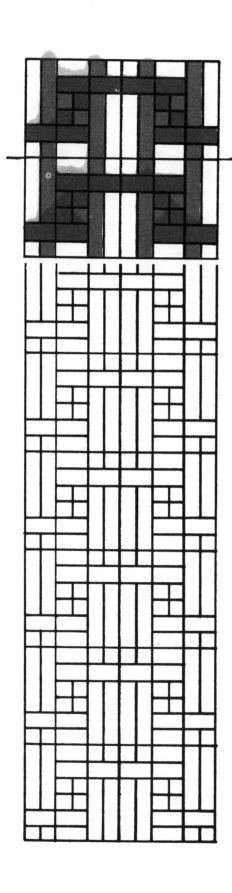

Design No. 25

Border Size   18   inches in width
Pattern Repeat   9   inches
Quilt Size   Full
Number of Repeats for entire Quilt   28
Frame Measurements:
   Side Panels: 4   inches by   116   inches
    Top and Bottom Panels: 4   inches by   98   inches
Corner Measurements: 18   inches square

Color	Number of templates in repeat	Number of templates in total border	Template code
Purple	4	112	S1
	8	224	R1
Red	8	224	S1
	4	112	R3
White	4	112	S1
	4	112	R1
	4	112	R3
Total	**36**	**1,008**	

Design No. 26

Border Size   18   inches in width
Pattern Repeat   9   inches
Quilt Size   Full
Number of Repeats for entire Quilt   28
Frame Measurements:
  Side Panels: 4   inches by   116   inches
  Top and Bottom Panels: 4   inches by   98   inches
Corner Measurements: 18   inches square

Color	Number of templates in repeat	Number of templates in total border	Template code
Red	2	56	S7
Orange	8	224	T1
Gold	4	112	R1
Blue	4	112	R1
Green	4	112	R1
Brown	4	112	R1
Pink	8	224	S1
	4	112	R1
White	8	224	S1
	16	448	T1
Total	**62**	**1,736**	

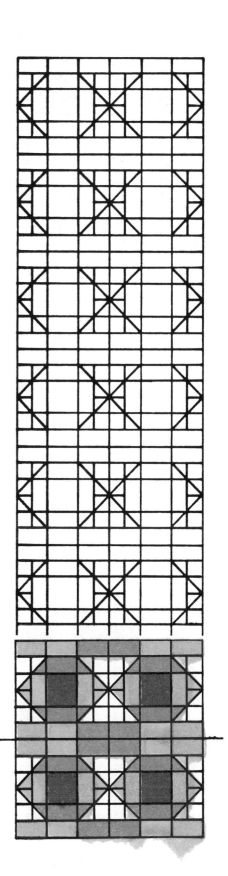

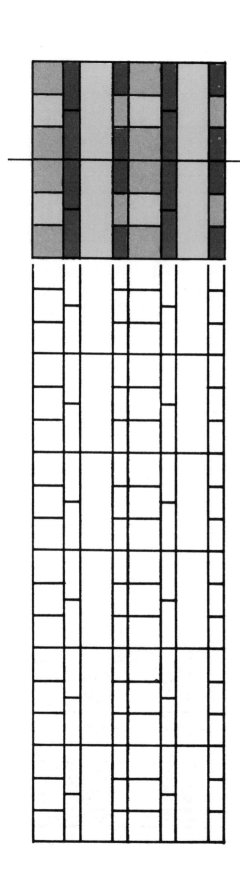

Design No. 27

Border Size   18   inches in width
Pattern Repeat   9   inches
Quilt Size   Full
Number of Repeats for entire Quilt   28
Frame Measurements:
   Side Panels: 4   inches by   116   inches
      Top and Bottom Panels: 4   inches by   98   inches
Corner Measurements: 18   inches square

Color	Number of templates in repeat	Number of templates in total border	Template code
Pink	2	56	R1
	2	56	R2
Brown	2	56	R1
	2	56	R2
Green	4	112	S7
	2	56	R1
Beige	2	56	S7
	2	56	R53
Total	**18**	**504**	

Design No. 28

Border Size 18 inches in width
Pattern Repeat 9 inches
Quilt Size Full
Number of Repeats for entire Quilt 28
Frame Measurements:
  Side Panels: 4 inches by 116 inches
   Top and Bottom Panels: 4 inches by 98 inches
Corner Measurements: 18 inches square

Color	Number of templates in repeat	Number of templates in total border	Template code
Red	6	168	R1
Black	6	168	R1
Yellow	3	84	R50
White	3	84	R50
Total	**18**	**504**	

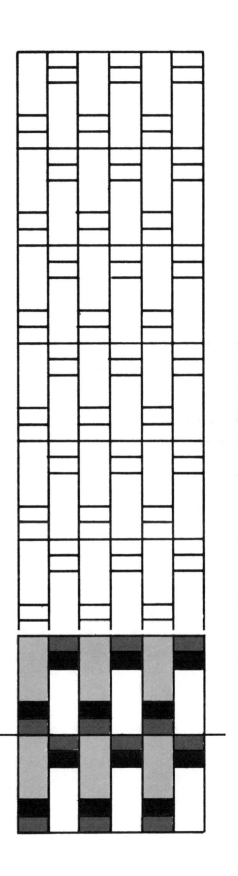

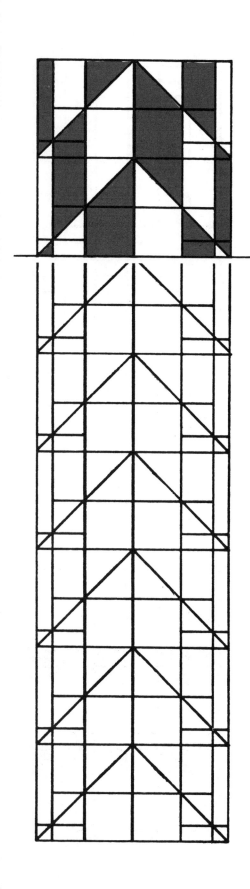

Design No. 29

Border Size   18   inches in width
Pattern Repeat   18   inches
Quilt Size   Full
Number of Repeats for entire Quilt   14
Frame Measurements:
   Side Panels: 4   inches by   116   inches
   Top and Bottom Panels: 4   inches by   98   inches
Corner Measurements: 18   inches square

Color	Number of templates in repeat	Number of templates in total border	Template code
Red	2	28	S13
	4	56	T1
	4	56	T7
	4	56	T15
	2	28	R1
	2	28	R4
	2	28	R49
White	2	28	S13
	4	56	T7
	4	56	T15
	2	28	R1
	2	28	R4
	2	28	R49
	2	28	T1
Total	**40**	**560**	

Design No. 30

Border Size 18 inches in width
Pattern Repeat 18 inches
Quilt Size Full
Number of Repeats for entire Quilt 14
Frame Measurements:
    Side Panels: 4 inches by 116 inches
    Top and Bottom Panels: 4 inches by 98 inches
Corner Measurements: 18 inches square

Color	Number of templates in repeat	Number of templates in total border	Template code
Yellow	4	56	T22
White	20	280	T7
Turquoise	12	168	S7
	12	168	T7
Total	**48**	**672**	

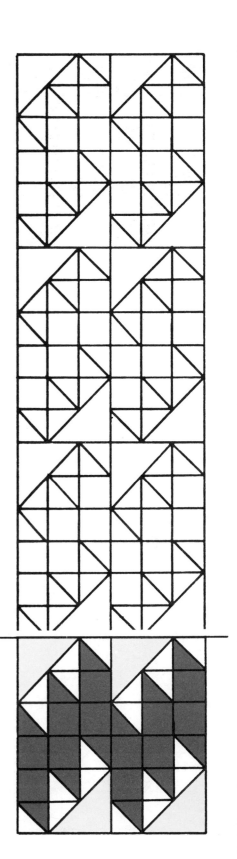

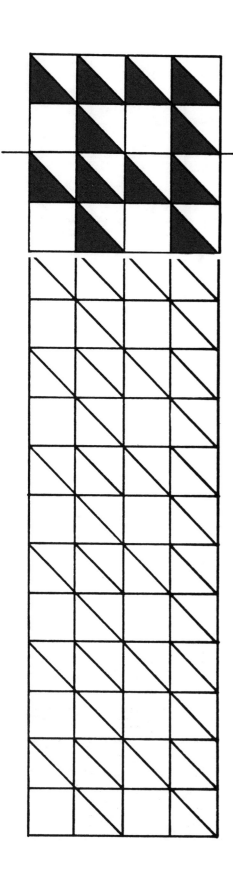

Design No. 31

Border Size 18 inches in width
Pattern Repeat 9 inches
Quilt Size Full
Number of Repeats for entire Quilt 28
Frame Measurements:
   Side Panels: 4 inches by 116 inches
    Top and Bottom Panels: 4 inches by 98 inches
Corner Measurements: 18 inches square

Color	Number of templates in repeat	Number of templates in total border	Template code
Purple	6	168	T15
White	2	56	S13
	6	168	T15
Total	**14**	**392**	

152

Design No. 32

Border Size 18 inches in width
Pattern Repeat 9 inches
Quilt Size Full
Number of Repeats for entire Quilt 28
Frame Measurements:
    Side Panels: 4 inches by 116 inches
    Top and Bottom Panels: 4 inches by 98 inches
Corner Measurements: 18 inches square

Color	Number of templates in repeat	Number of templates in total border	Template code
Pink	12	336	S1
Purple	6	168	S7
White	12	336	S1
	12	336	R1
Total	**42**	**1,176**	

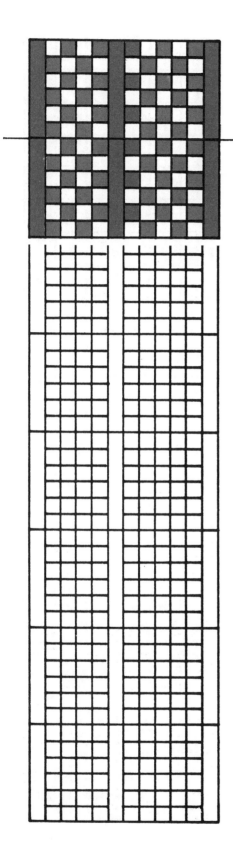

Design No. 33

Border Size   18   inches in width
Pattern Repeat   9   inches
Quilt Size   Full
Number of Repeats for entire Quilt   28
Frame Measurements:
   Side Panels: 4   inches by   116   inches
      Top and Bottom Panels: 4   inches by   98   inches
Corner Measurements: 18   inches square

Color	Number of templates in repeat	Number of templates in total border	Template code
White	30	840	S1
Orange	24	672	S1
Green	3	84	S1
	3	84	R5
Total	**60**	**1,680**	

Design No. 34

Border Size   18   inches in width
Pattern Repeat   9   inches
Quilt Size   Full
Number of Repeats for entire Quilt   28
Frame Measurements:
   Side Panels: 4   inches by   116   inches
   Top and Bottom Panels: 4   inches by   98   inches
Corner Measurements: 18   inches square

Color	Number of templates in repeat	Number of templates in total border	Template code
Pink	5	140	T7
Blue	5	140	T7
White	3	84	T7
Beige	4	56	R5
	2	56	R5
Brown	2	56	R5
	2	56	R7
Total	**23**	**644**	

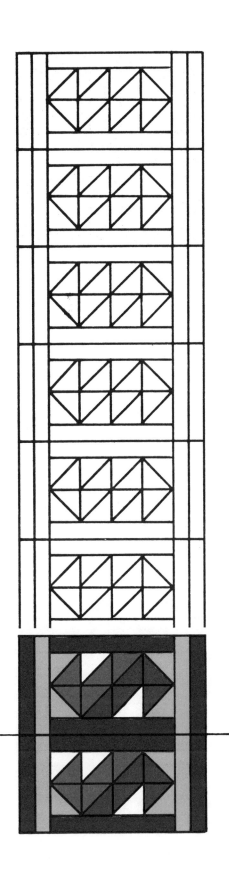

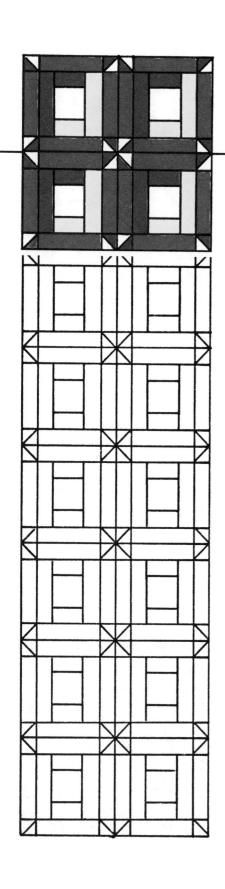

Design No. 35

Border Size 18 inches in width
Pattern Repeat 9 inches
Quilt Size Full
Number of Repeats for entire Quilt 28
Frame Measurements:
    Side Panels: 4 inches by 116 inches
    Top and Bottom Panels: 4 inches by 98 inches
Corner Measurements: 18 inches square

Color	Number of templates in repeat	Number of templates in total border	Template code
Red	8	224	R3
White	2	56	S7
	8	224	T1
Yellow	2	56	R1
	2	56	R3
Blue	8	224	T1
	2	56	R1
	2	56	R3
Total	**34**	**952**	

Design No. 36

Border Size   18   inches in width
Pattern Repeat   9   inches
Quilt Size   Full
Number of Repeats for entire Quilt   28
Frame Measurements:
   Side Panels: 4   inches by   116   inches
   Top and Bottom Panels: 4   inches by   98   inches
Corner Measurements: 18   inches square

Color	Number of templates in repeat	Number of templates in total border	Template code
White	32	896	T1
	2	56	R50
Purple	32	896	T1
	2	56	R5
	1	28	R53
Total	**69**	**1,932**	

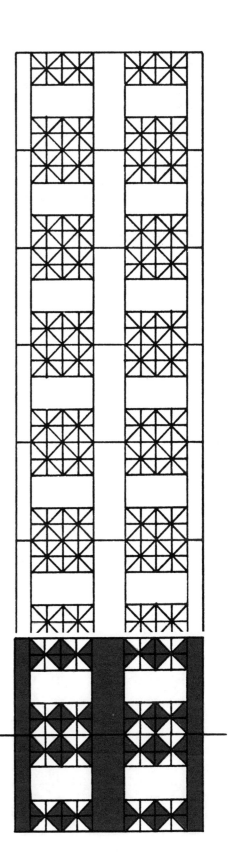

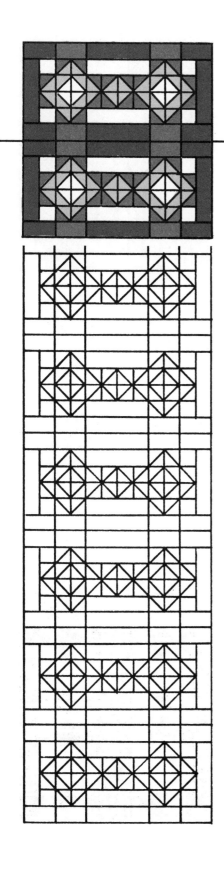

Design No. 37

Border Size   18   inches in width
Pattern Repeat   9   inches
Quilt Size   Full
Number of Repeats for entire Quilt   28
Frame Measurements:
   Side Panels: 4   inches by   116   inches
    Top and Bottom Panels: 4   inches by   98   inches
Corner Measurements: 18   inches square

Color	Number of templates in repeat	Number of templates in total border	Template code
Light Green	28	784	T1
Dark Green	20	560	T1
	4	112	R1
White	4	112	S1
	2	56	R3
Brown	4	112	R1
	4	112	R3
Total	**66**	**1,848**	

Design No. 38

Border Size   18   inches in width
Pattern Repeat   9   inches
Quilt Size   Full
Number of Repeats for entire Quilt   28
Frame Measurements:
   Side Panels: 4   inches by   116   inches
   Top and Bottom Panels: 4   inches by   98   inches
Corner Measurements: 18   inches square

Color	Number of templates in repeat	Number of templates in total border	Template code
White	16	448	T1
Orange	16	448	T1
Red	4	112	S7
	8	224	T7
Blue	8	224	T7
	4	112	R1
Total	**56**	**1,568**	

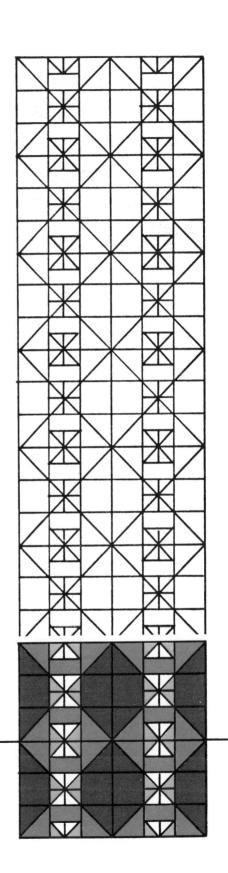

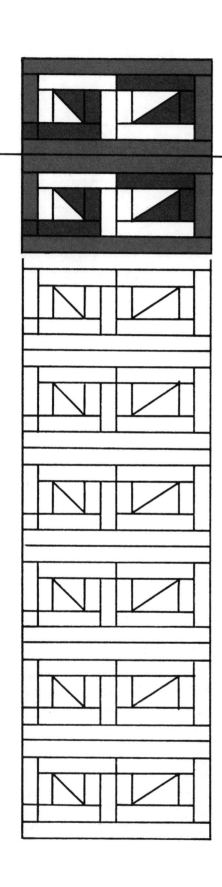

Design No. 39

Border Size 18 inches in width
Pattern Repeat 9 inches
Quilt Size Full
Number of Repeats for entire Quilt 28
Frame Measurements:
  Side Panels: 4 inches by 116 inches
   Top and Bottom Panels: 4 inches by 98 inches
Corner Measurements: 18 inches square

Color	Number of templates in repeat	Number of templates in total border	Template code
Red	2	56	R2
	2	56	R3
	2	56	R11
White	1	28	T7
	1	28	T11
	2	56	R1
	1	28	R2
	2	56	R4
Purple	1	28	S1
	1	28	T7
	1	28	T11
	2	56	R1
	1	28	R3
	1	28	R4
Total	**20**	**560**	

Design No. 40

Border Size   18   inches in width
Pattern Repeat   18   inches
Quilt Size   Full
Number of Repeats for entire Quilt   14
Frame Measurements:
    Side Panels: 4   inches by   116   inches
    Top and Bottom Panels: 4   inches by   98   inches
Corner Measurements: 18   inches square

Color	Number of templates in repeat	Number of templates in total border	Template code
Gold	16	224	S1
	4	56	T1
Blue	4	56	S1
	9	126	S7
	16	224	T1
White	24	336	S1
	4	56	S7
	16	224	T1
	12	168	R1
Total	**105**	**1,470**	

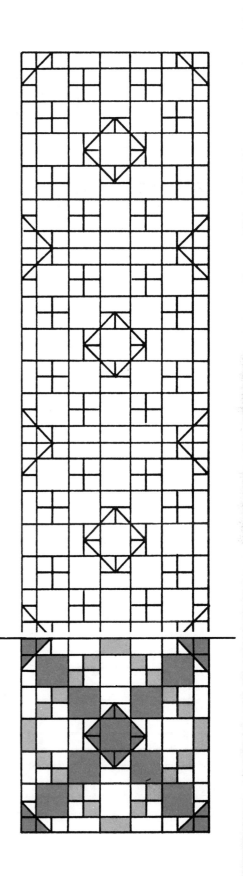

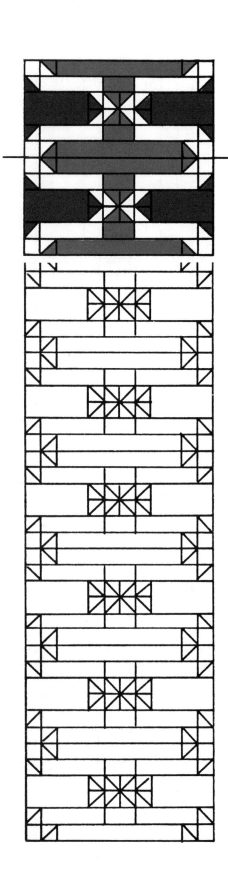

Design No. 41

Border Size 18 inches in width
Pattern Repeat 9 inches
Quilt Size Full
Number of Repeats for entire Quilt 28
Frame Measurements:
  Side Panels: 4 inches by 116 inches
   Top and Bottom Panels: 4 inches by 98 inches
Corner Measurements: 18 inches square

Color	Number of templates in repeat	Number of templates in total border	Template code
Dark Purple	8	224	T1
	2	56	R50
Light Purple	8	224	T1
	2	56	R1
	2	56	R7
White	4	112	S1
	16	448	T1
	4	112	R3
Total	**46**	**1,288**	

Design No. 42

Border Size 18 inches in width
Pattern Repeat 9 inches
Quilt Size Full
Number of Repeats for entire Quilt 28
Frame Measurements:
  Side Panels: 4 inches by 116 inches
  Top and Bottom Panels: 4 inches by 98 inches
Corner Measurements: 18 inches square

Color	Number of templates in repeat	Number of templates in total border	Template code
Pink	12	336	S1
	2	56	R1
White	3	84	S7
	6	168	R1
Green	12	336	S1
	10	280	R1
Total	**45**	**1,260**	

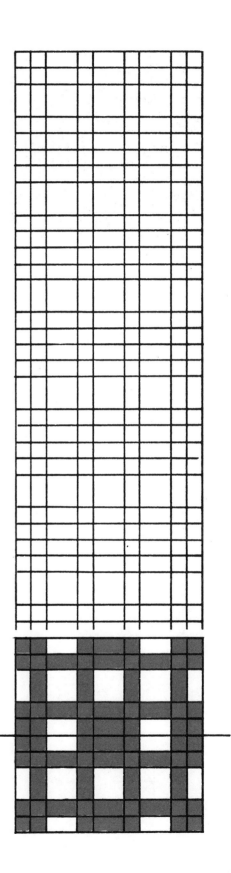

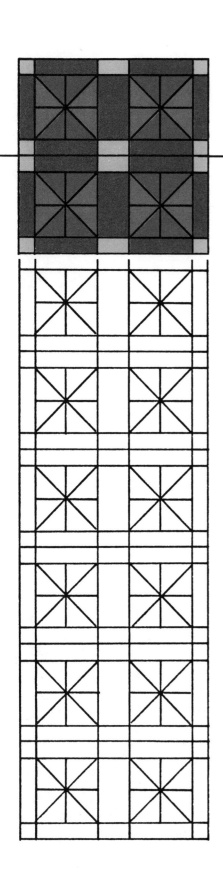

Design No. 43

Border Size 18 inches in width
Pattern Repeat 9 inches
Quilt Size Full
Number of Repeats for entire Quilt 28
Frame Measurements:
  Side Panels: 4 inches by 116 inches
   Top and Bottom Panels: 4 inches by 98 inches
Corner Measurements: 18 inches square

Color	Number of templates in repeat	Number of templates in total border	Template code
Blue	8	224	T7
Dark Pink	8	224	T7
Brown	6	168	R3
	1	28	R50
Light Pink	4	112	S1
	2	56	R1
Total	**29**	**784**	

Design No. 44

Border Size   18   inches in width
Pattern Repeat   18   inches
Quilt Size   Full
Number of Repeats for entire Quilt   14
Frame Measurements:
   Side Panels: 4   inches by   116   inches
   Top and Bottom Panels: 4   inches by   98   inches
Corner Measurements: 18   inches square

Color	Number of templates in repeat	Number of templates in total border	Template code
Red	16	448	R1
	8	224	R5
White	8	224	R1
	8	224	R5
Total	**40**	**1,120**	

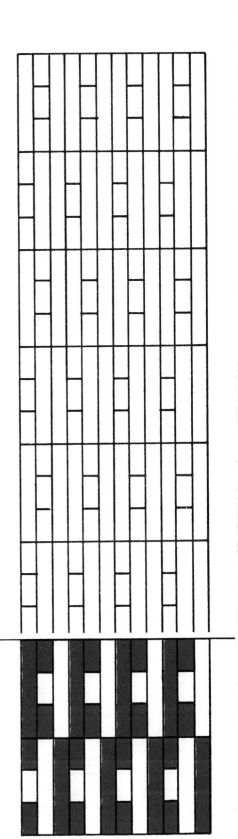

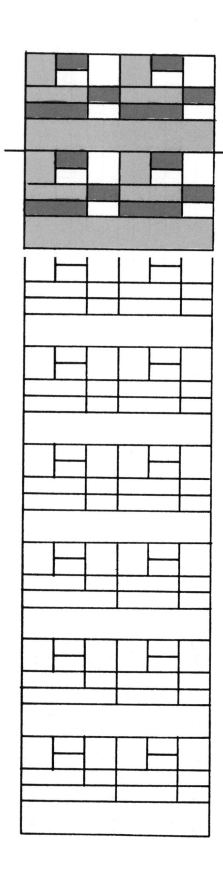

Design No. 45

Border Size   18   inches in width
Pattern Repeat   9   inches
Quilt Size   Full
Number of Repeats for entire Quilt   28
Frame Measurements:
   Side Panels: 4   inches by   116   inches
   Top and Bottom Panels: 4   inches by   98   inches
Corner Measurements: 18   inches square

Color	Number of templates in repeat	Number of templates in total border	Template code
Green	4	112	R1
	2	56	R3
White	2	56	S7
	4	112	R1
Gold	2	56	S7
	2	56	R3
	1	28	R59
Total	**17**	**476**	

Design No. 46

Border Size 18 inches in width
Pattern Repeat 9 inches
Quilt Size Full
Number of Repeats for entire Quilt 28
Frame Measurements:
    Side Panels: 4 inches by 116 inches
    Top and Bottom Panels: 4 inches by 98 inches
Corner Measurements: 18 inches square

Color	Number of templates in repeat	Number of templates in total border	Template code
White	4	112	S7
Brown	6	168	S7
Red	4	112	R50
Total	**14**	**392**	

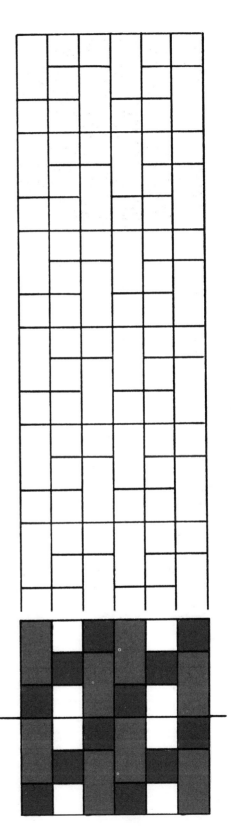

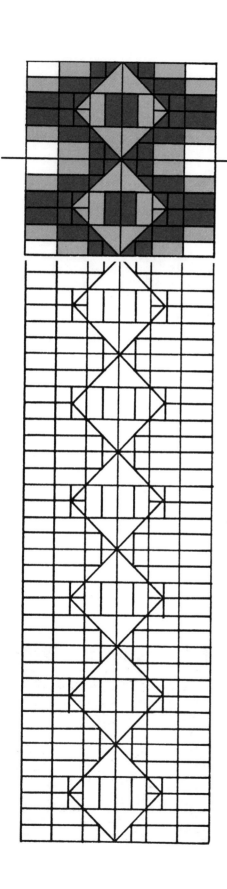

Design No. 47

Border Size 18 inches in width
Pattern Repeat 9 inches
Quilt Size Full
Number of Repeats for entire Quilt 28
Frame Measurements:
   Side Panels: 4 inches by 116 inches
    Top and Bottom Panels: 4 inches by 98 inches
Corner Measurements: 18 inches square

Color	Number of templates in repeat	Number of templates in total border	Template code
White	4	112	R1
Green	4	112	T1
	4	112	T7
	10	280	R1
Blue	8	224	S1
	12	336	T1
	10	280	R1
Total	**52**	**1,456**	

Design No. 48

Border Size 18 inches in width
Pattern Repeat 9 inches
Quilt Size Full
Number of Repeats for entire Quilt 28
Frame Measurements:
   Side Panels: 4 inches by 116 inches
   Top and Bottom Panels: 4 inches by 98 inches
Corner Measurements: 18 inches square

Color	Number of templates in repeat	Number of templates in total border	Template code
Dark Pink	2	56	S7
Pink	4	112	R50
White	4	112	S7
	2	56	R50
Total	**12**	**336**	

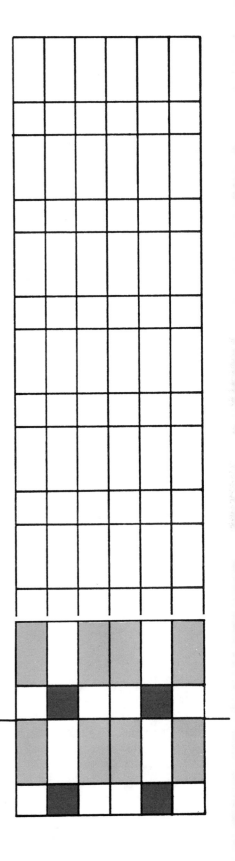

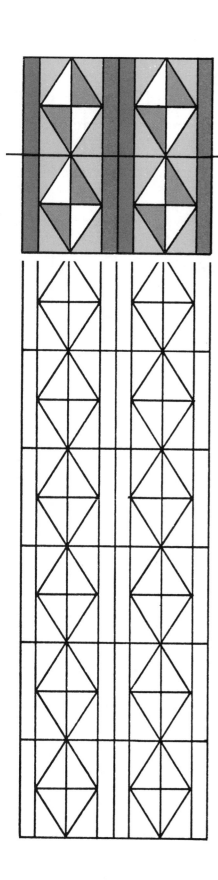

Design No. 49

Border Size   18   inches in width
Pattern Repeat   9   inches
Quilt Size   Full
Number of Repeats for entire Quilt   28
Frame Measurements:
   Side Panels: 4   inches by   116   inches
   Top and Bottom Panels: 4· inches by   98   inches
Corner Measurements: 18   inches square

Color	Number of templates in repeat	Number of templates in total border	Template code
Blue	2	56	R5
Dark Pink	2	56	R5
Light Pink	8	224	T11
White	4	112	T11
Gray	2	56	T11
Total	**18**	**504**	

Design No. 50

Border Size 18 inches in width
Pattern Repeat 18 inches
Quilt Size Full
Number of Repeats for entire Quilt 14
Frame Measurements:
  Side Panels: 4 inches by 116 inches
  Top and Bottom Panels: 4 inches by 98 inches
Corner Measurements: 18 inches square

Color	Number of templates in repeat	Number of templates in total border	Template code
Brown	2	28	R1
	4	56	R4
Green	2	28	R1
	2	28	R4
	2	28	R95
White	2	28	R4
	2	28	R50
	2	28	R95
Total	**18**	**252**	

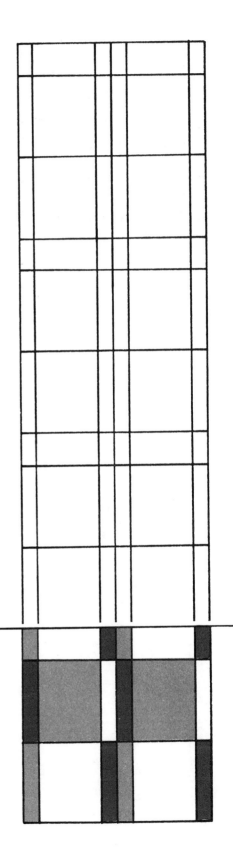

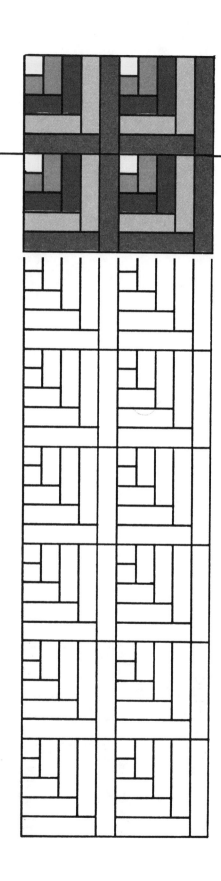

Design No. 51

Border Size 20 inches in width
Pattern Repeat 10 inches
Quilt Size Queen
Number of Repeats for entire Quilt 28
Frame Measurements:
   Side Panels: 2 inches by 124 inches
    Top and Bottom Panels: 2 inches by 104 inches
Corner Measurements: 20 inches square

Color	Number of templates in repeat	Number of templates in total border	Template code
Yellow	2	56	S3
Orange	2	56	S3
	2	56	R25
Brown	2	56	R25
	2	56	R27
Light Green	2	56	R27
	2	56	R29
Dark Green	2	56	R29
	2	56	R31
Total	**18**	**504**	

Design No. 52

Border Size 20 inches in width
Pattern Repeat 20 inches
Quilt Size Queen
Number of Repeats for entire Quilt 14
Frame Measurements:
  Side Panels: 2 inches by 124 inches
  Top and Bottom Panels: 2 inches by 104 inches
Corner Measurements: 20 inches square

Color	Number of templates in repeat	Number of templates in total border	Template code
White	8	112	R25
Gray	8	112	S3
	4	56	R25
Blue	2	28	S3
	1	14	R25
	4	56	R27
	2	28	R29
	2	28	R31
Fuchsia	2	28	S3
	1	14	R25
	4	56	R27
	2	28	R29
	2	28	R31
Total	**42**	**588**	

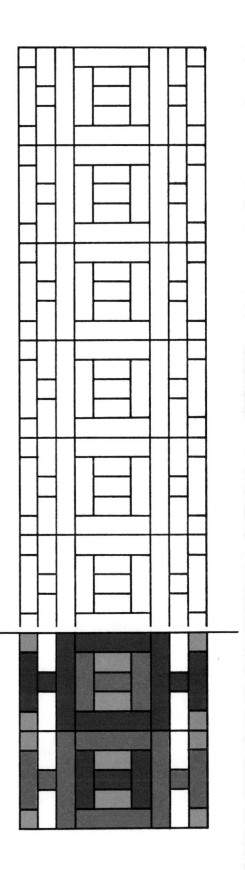

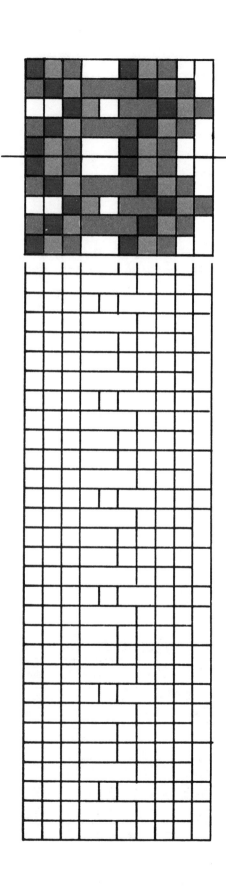

Design No. 53

Border Size   20   inches in width
Pattern Repeat   10   inches
Quilt Size   Queen
Number of Repeats for entire Quilt   28
Frame Measurements:
   Side Panels: 2   inches by   124   inches
      Top and Bottom Panels: 2   inches by   104   inches
Corner Measurements: 20   inches square

Color	Number of templates in repeat	Number of templates in total border	Template code
Pink	10	280	S3
Green	10	280	S3
Gray	9	250	S3
	1	28	R25
	2	56	R27
White	5	140	S3
	4	112	R25
Total	**41**	**1,148**	

Design No. 54

Border Size 20 inches in width
Pattern Repeat 10 inches
Quilt Size Queen
Number of Repeats for entire Quilt 28
Frame Measurements:
  Side Panels: 2 inches by 124 inches
  Top and Bottom Panels: 2 inches by 104 inches
Corner Measurements: 20 inches square

Color	Number of templates in repeat	Number of templates in total border	Template code
Green	5	140	R27
Brown	10	280	S3
White	10	280	S3
	5	140	R27
Total	**30**	**840**	

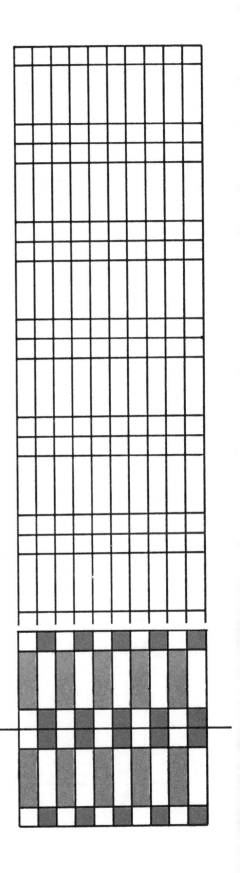

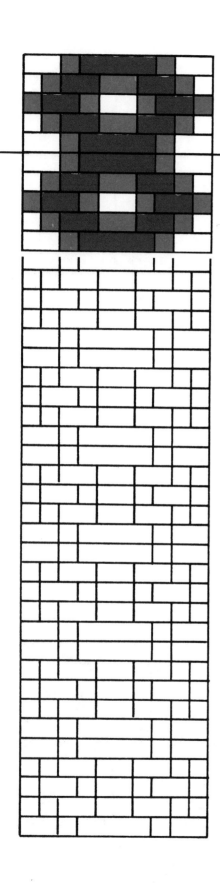

Design No. 55

Border Size 20 inches in width
Pattern Repeat 10 inches
Quilt Size Queen
Number of Repeats for entire Quilt 28
Frame Measurements:
   Side Panels: 2 inches by 124 inches
   Top and Bottom Panels: 2 inches by 104 inches
Corner Measurements: 20 inches square

Color	Number of templates in repeat	Number of templates in total border	Template code
Blue	12	336	S3
	2	56	R25
White	4	112	S3
	5	140	R25
Purple	6	168	R25
	2	56	R29
Total	**31**	**868**	

Design No. 56

Border Size   20   inches in width
Pattern Repeat   20   inches
Quilt Size   Queen
Number of Repeats for entire Quilt   14
Frame Measurements:
  Side Panels: 2   inches by   124   inches
  Top and Bottom Panels: 2   inches by   104   inches
Corner Measurements: 20   inches square

Color	Number of templates in repeat	Number of templates in total border	Template code
White	4	56	R25
	4	56	R96
Green	4	56	R27
	4	56	R72
Total	**16**	**224**	

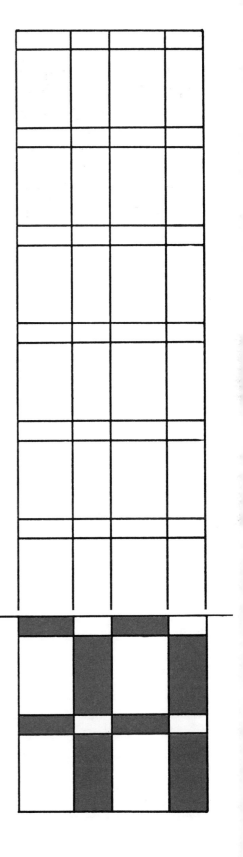

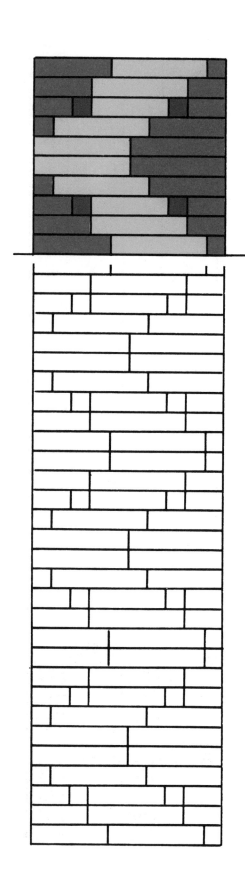

Design No. 57

Border Size 20 inches in width
Pattern Repeat 20 inches
Quilt Size Queen
Number of Repeats for entire Quilt 14
Frame Measurements:
  Side Panels: 2 inches by 124 inches
  Top and Bottom Panels: 2 inches by 104 inches
Corner Measurements: 20 inches square

Color	Number of templates in repeat	Number of templates in total border	Template code
Red	4	56	S3
Beige	8	112	R31
	2	28	R29
Blue	4	46	S3
	6	84	R25
	2	28	R27
	4	56	R29
	2	28	R31
Total	**30**	**420**	

Design No. 58

Border Size 20 inches in width
Pattern Repeat 10 inches
Quilt Size Queen
Number of Repeats for entire Quilt 28
Frame Measurements:
   Side Panels: 2 inches by 124 inches
    Top and Bottom Panels: 2 inches by 104 inches
Corner Measurements: 20 inches square

Color	Number of templates in repeat	Number of templates in total border	Template code
Yellow	8	224	T13
Green	8	224	T13
Orange	4	112	S3
	2	56	R25
White	6	168	R27
	1	28	R71
Total	**29**	**812**	

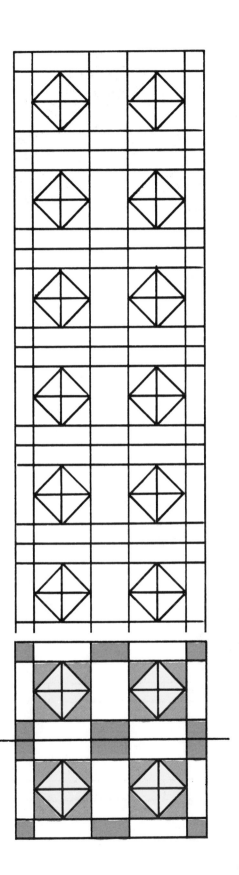

Design No. 59

Border Size 20 inches in width
Pattern Repeat 20 inches
Quilt Size Queen
Number of Repeats for entire Quilt 14
Frame Measurements:
    Side Panels: 2 inches by 124 inches
    Top and Bottom Panels: 2 inches by 104 inches
Corner Measurements: 20 inches square

Color	Number of templates in repeat	Number of templates in total border	Template code
Blue	2	28	S3
	3	42	R25
	2	28	R27
	3	42	R29
	1	14	R32
	1	14	R34
	1	14	R36
Brown	2	28	S3
	3	42	R25
	2	28	R27
	3	42	R29
	1	14	R32
	1	14	R34
	1	14	R36
Total	**26**	**364**	

Design No. 60

Border Size 20 inches in width
Pattern Repeat 10 inches
Quilt Size Queen
Number of Repeats for entire Quilt 28
Frame Measurements:
  Side Panels: 2 inches by 124 inches
  Top and Bottom Panels: 2 inches by 104 inches
Corner Measurements: 20 inches square

Color	Number of templates in repeat	Number of templates in total border	Template code
White	30	840	T3
Blue	30	840	T3
Purple	2	56	T32
Total	**62**	**1,736**	

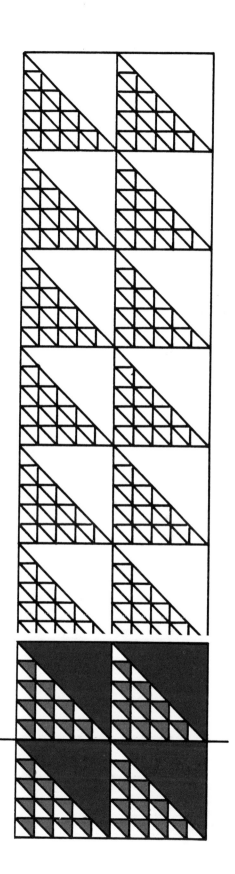

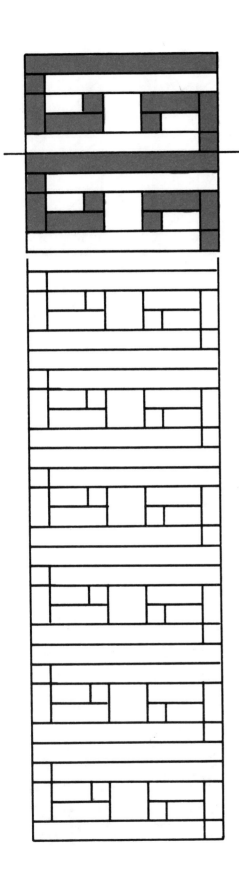

Design No. 61

Border Size 20 inches in width
Pattern Repeat 10 inches
Quilt Size Queen
Number of Repeats for entire Quilt 28
Frame Measurements:
  Side Panels: 2 inches by 124 inches
   Top and Bottom Panels: 2 inches by 104 inches
Corner Measurements: 20 inches square

Color	Number of templates in repeat	Number of templates in total border	Template code
Blue	4	112	S3
	2	56	R25
	2	56	R27
	1	28	R36
White	2	56	R25
	1	28	S11
	2	56	R35
Total	**14**	**392**	

Design No. 62

Border Size   20   inches in width
Pattern Repeat   10   inches
Quilt Size   Queen
Number of Repeats for entire Quilt   28
Frame Measurements:
   Side Panels: 2   inches by   124   inches
   Top and Bottom Panels: 2   inches by   104   inches
Corner Measurements: 20   inches square

Color	Number of templates in repeat	Number of templates in total border	Template code
White	2	56	S3
Maroon	6	168	R25
	1	28	R29
Pink	4	112	S11
	2	56	R72
Total	**15**	**420**	

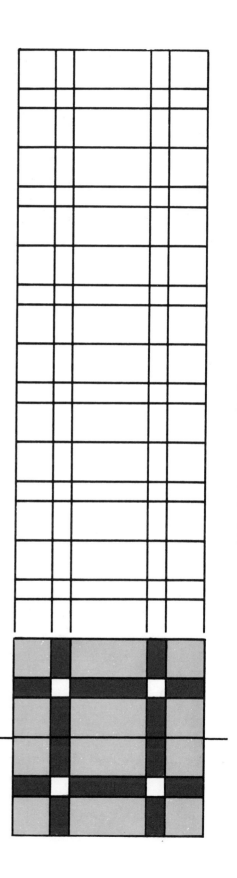

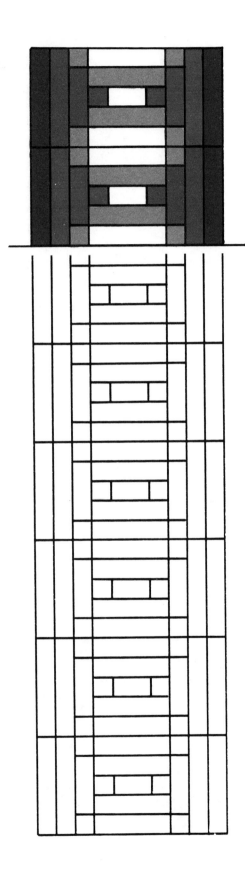

Design No. 63

Border Size   20   inches in width
Pattern Repeat   20   inches
Quilt Size   Queen
Number of Repeats for entire Quilt   14
Frame Measurements:
  Side Panels: 2   inches by   124   inches
  Top and Bottom Panels: 2   inches by   104   inches
Corner Measurements: 20   inches square

Color	Number of templates in repeat	Number of templates in total border	Template code
Purple	4	56	R31
White	2	28	R25
	4	56	R29
Green	8	112	S3
	4	56	R29
Pink	2	28	S3
	2	28	R27
	2	28	R31
Brown	2	28	S3
	2	28	R27
	2	28	R31
Total	**34**	**476**	

Design No. 64

Border Size   20   inches in width
Pattern Repeat   10   inches
Quilt Size   Queen
Number of Repeats for entire Quilt   28
Frame Measurements:
   Side Panels: 2   inches by   124   inches
    Top and Bottom Panels: 2   inches by   104   inches
Corner Measurements: 20   inches square

Color	Number of templates in repeat	Number of templates in total border	Template code
White	6	168	S3
	2	56	R29
Yellow	6	168	S3
	4	112	T13
	1	28	R29
Green	2	56	S3
	4	112	T13
	2	56	R29
Total	**27**	**756**	

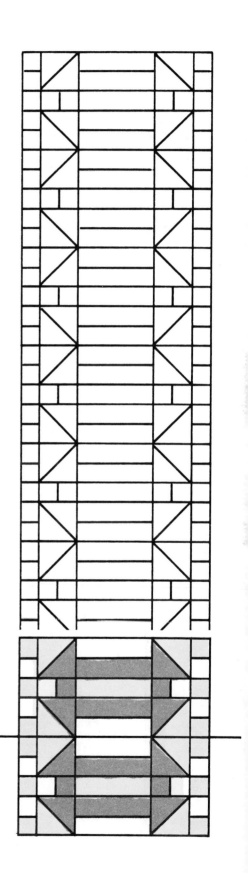

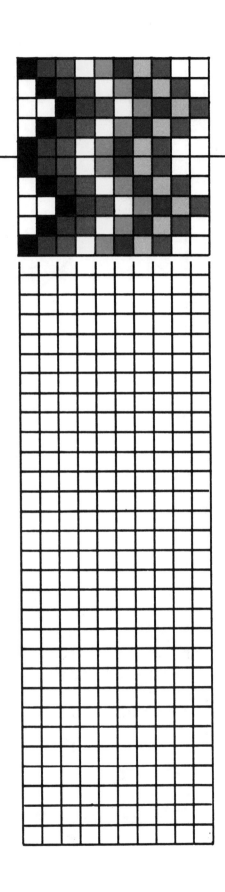

Design No. 65

Border Size   20   inches in width
Pattern Repeat   10   inches
Quilt Size   Queen
Number of Repeats for entire Quilt   28
Frame Measurements:
   Side Panels: 2   inches by   124   inches
   Top and Bottom Panels: 2   inches by   104   inches
Corner Measurements: 20   inches square

Color	Number of templates in repeat	Number of templates in total border	Template code
White	10	280	S3
Pink	5	140	S3
Green	5	140	S3
Purple	5	140	S3
Blue	5	140	S3
Yellow	5	140	S3
Red	5	140	S3
Brown	5	140	S3
Black	5	140	S3
Total	**50**	**1,400**	

Design No. 66

Border Size   20   inches in width
Pattern Repeat   10   inches
Quilt Size   Queen
Number of Repeats for entire Quilt   28
Frame Measurements:
   Side Panels: 2   inches by   124   inches
    Top and Bottom Panels: 2   inches by   104   inches
Corner Measurements: 20   inches square

Color	Number of templates in repeat	Number of templates in total border	Template code
White	6	168	S3
	2	56	R25
Light Green	6	168	S3
	10	280	R25
Dark Green	2	56	S3
	1	28	R25
	2	56	R31
Total	**29**	**812**	

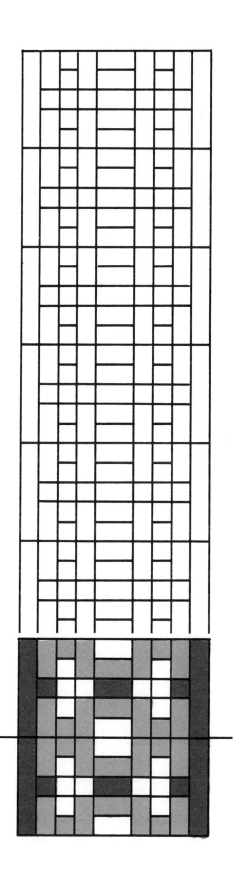

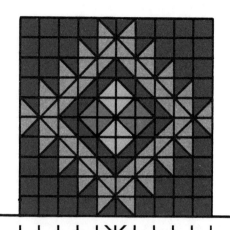

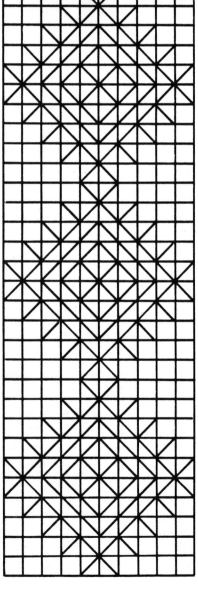

Design No. 67

Border Size   20   inches in width
Pattern Repeat   20   inches
Quilt Size   Queen
Number of Repeats for entire Quilt   14
Frame Measurements:
  Side Panels: 2   inches by   124   inches
   Top and Bottom Panels: 2   inches by   104   inches
Corner Measurements: 20   inches square

Color	Number of templates in repeat	Number of templates in total border	Template code
Yellow	8	112	T3
Blue	8	112	T3
Green	64	896	T3
Henna	40	560	S3
	40	560	T3
Total	**160**	**2,240**	

Design No. 68

Border Size 20 inches in width
Pattern Repeat 10 inches
Quilt Size Queen
Number of Repeats for entire Quilt 28
Frame Measurements:
   Side Panels: 2 inches by 124 inches
    Top and Bottom Panels: 2 inches by 104 inches
Corner Measurements: 20 inches square

Color	Number of templates in repeat	Number of templates in total border	Template code
Dark Blue	2	56	S3
	4	112	R27
	2	56	R31
Light Blue	8	224	S3
	4	112	R25
	2	56	R31
Total	**22**	**616**	

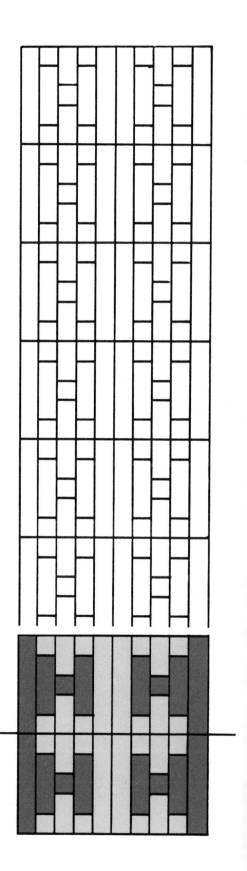

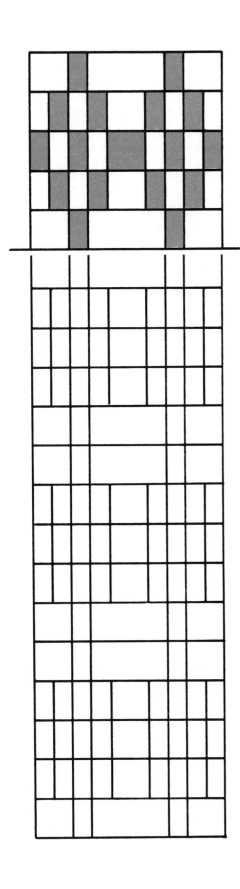

Design No. 69

Border Size   20   inches in width
Pattern Repeat   20   inches
Quilt Size   Queen
Number of Repeats for entire Quilt   14
Frame Measurements:
    Side Panels: 2   inches by   124   inches
    Top and Bottom Panels: 2   inches by   104   inches
Corner Measurements: 20   inches square

Color	Number of templates in repeat	Number of templates in total border	Template code
Green	1	14	S11
	16	224	R25
White	6	84	S11
	12	168	R25
	2	28	R72
Total	**37**	**518**	

Design No. 70

Border Size   20   inches in width
Pattern Repeat   20   inches
Quilt Size   Queen
Number of Repeats for entire Quilt   14
Frame Measurements:
    Side Panels: 2   inches by   124   inches
    Top and Bottom Panels: 2   inches by   104   inches
Corner Measurements: 20   inches square

Color	Number of templates in repeat	Number of templates in total border	Template code
Purple	16	224	S3
	1	14	S11
Brown	2	28	S11
	2	28	R25
White	16	224	S3
	10	140	S11
	6	84	R25
Total	**53**	**742**	

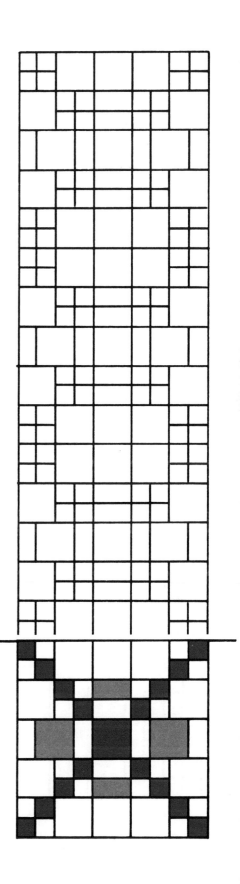

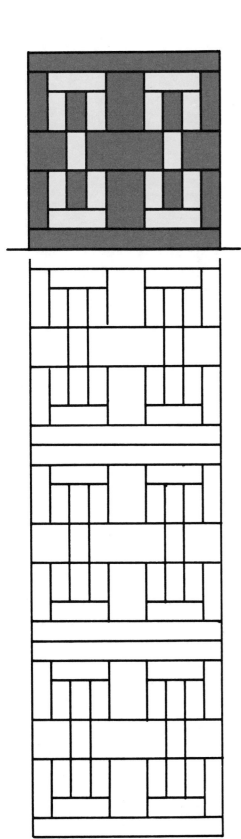

Design No. 71

Border Size   20   inches in width
Pattern Repeat   20   inches
Quilt Size   Queen
Number of Repeats for entire Quilt   14
Frame Measurements:
   Side Panels: 2   inches by   124   inches
   Top and Bottom Panels: 2   inches by   104   inches
Corner Measurements: 20   inches square

Color	Number of templates in repeat	Number of templates in total border	Template code
Yellow	10	140	R25
	4	56	R27
Orange	2	28	S11
	4	56	R25
	4	56	R27
	2	28	R36
	2	28	R71
Total	**28**	**392**	

Design No. 72

Border Size   20   inches in width
Pattern Repeat   10   inches
Quilt Size   Queen
Number of Repeats for entire Quilt   28
Frame Measurements:
   Side Panels: 2   inches by   124   inches
   Top and Bottom Panels: 2   inches by   104   inches
Corner Measurements: 20   inches square

Color	Number of templates in repeat	Number of templates in total border	Template code
Beige	2	56	S11
Red	2	56	R25
	2	56	R27
Brown	2	56	R27
	2	56	R29
Blue	2	56	R29
	2	56	R31
Total	**16**	**448**	

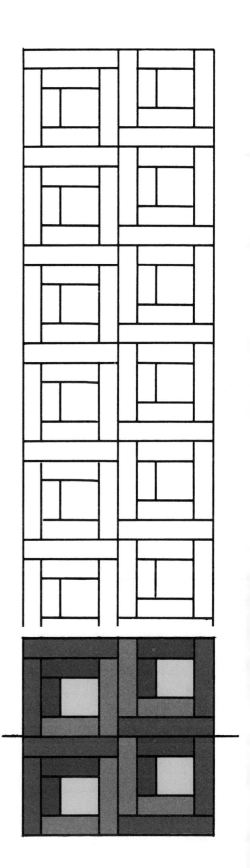

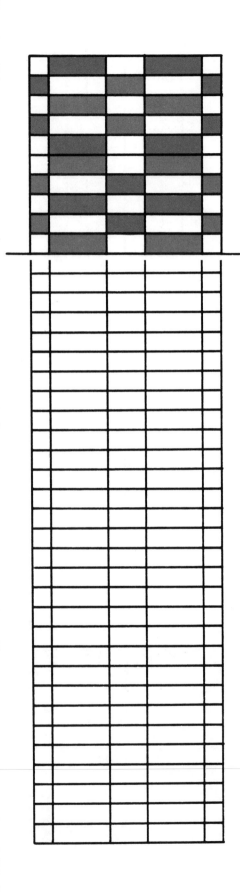

Design No. 73

Border Size   20   inches in width
Pattern Repeat   20   inches
Quilt Size   Queen
Number of Repeats for entire Quilt   14
Frame Measurements:
  Side Panels: 2   inches by   124   inches
  Top and Bottom Panels: 2   inches by   104   inches
Corner Measurements: 20   inches square

Color	Number of templates in repeat	Number of templates in total border	Template code
Blue	4	56	S3
	2	28	R25
	6	84	R27
Orange	4	56	S3
	2	28	R25
	6	84	R27
White	12	168	S3
	6	84	R25
	8	112	R27
Total	**50**	**700**	

Design No. 74

Border Size 20 inches in width
Pattern Repeat 20 inches
Quilt Size Queen
Number of Repeats for entire Quilt 14
Frame Measurements:
   Side Panels: 2 inches by 124 inches
    Top and Bottom Panels: 2 inches by 104 inches
Corner Measurements: 20 inches square

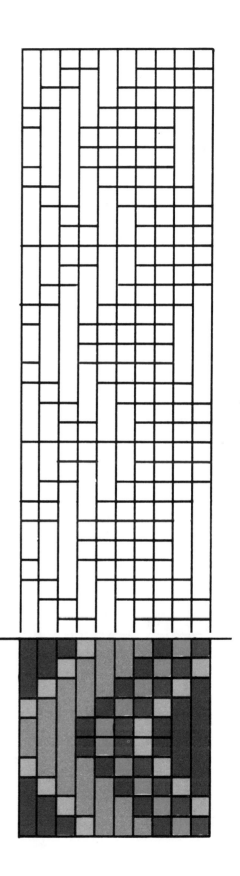

Color	Number of templates in repeat	Number of templates in total border	Template code
Yellow	16	224	S3
Pink	10	140	S3
Blue	10	140	S3
Henna	14	196	S3
	2	28	R25
	2	28	R27
	1	14	R29
	1	14	R32
Green	2	28	S3
	3	42	R25
	4	56	R27
	1	14	R29
	1	14	R32
Total	**67**	**938**	

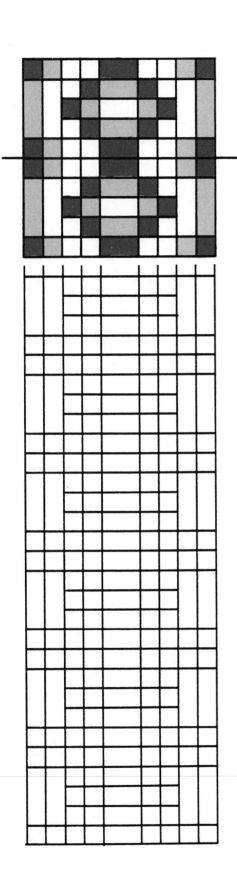

Design No. 75

Border Size   20   inches in width
Pattern Repeat   10   inches
Quilt Size   Queen
Number of Repeats for entire Quilt   28
Frame Measurements:
   Side Panels: 2   inches by   124   inches
   Top and Bottom Panels: 2   inches by   104   inches
Corner Measurements: 20   inches square

Color	Number of templates in repeat	Number of templates in total border	Template code
Henna	10	280	S3
	2	56	R25
Green	6	168	S3
	2	56	R25
	2	56	R27
White	12	336	S3
	1	28	R25
	2	56	R27
Total	**37**	**1,036**	

Design No. 76

Border Size   20   inches in width
Pattern Repeat   20   inches
Quilt Size   Queen
Number of Repeats for entire Quilt   14
Frame Measurements:
　　Side Panels: 2 inches by 124 inches
　　　Top and Bottom Panels: 2 inches by 104 inches
Corner Measurements: 20 inches square

Color	Number of templates in repeat	Number of templates in total border	Template code
Orange	12	168	S3
White	8	112	S3
	4	56	S11
	24	336	T3
Blue	16	224	S3
	1	14	S11
	24	336	T3
	8	112	R25
Total	**97**	**1,358**	

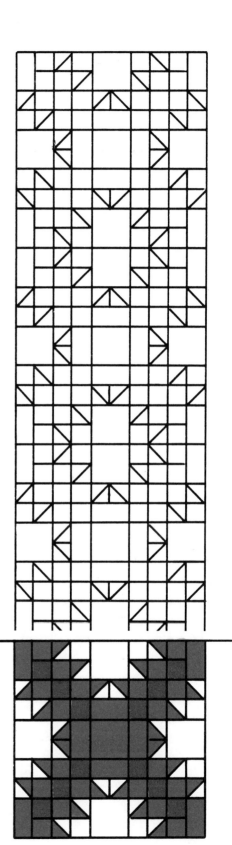

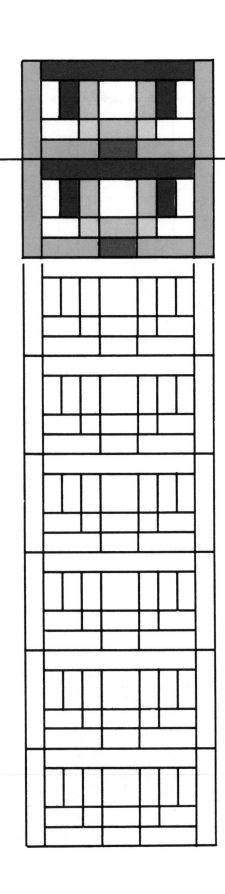

Design No. 77

Border Size   20   inches in width
Pattern Repeat   10   inches
Quilt Size   Queen
Number of Repeats for entire Quilt   28
Frame Measurements:
   Side Panels: 2   inches by   124   inches
   Top and Bottom Panels: 2   inches by   104   inches
Corner Measurements: 20   inches square

Color	Number of templates in repeat	Number of templates in total border	Template code
Red	1	28	R25
Green	2	56	S3
Gold	3	42	R25
Purple	2	56	R25
Brown	1	28	R34
Blue	2	56	R27
	2	56	R31
White	1	28	S11
	4	112	R25
Total	**18**	**504**	

Design No. 78

Border Size 20 inches in width
Pattern Repeat 10 inches
Quilt Size Queen
Number of Repeats for entire Quilt 28
Frame Measurements:
  Side Panels: 2 inches by 124 inches
  Top and Bottom Panels: 2 inches by 104 inches
Corner Measurements: 20 inches square

Color	Number of templates in repeat	Number of templates in total border	Template code
Yellow	6	168	S3
Pink	14	392	S3
White	18	504	S3
Green	2	56	S3
	2	56	R31
Total	**42**	**1,176**	

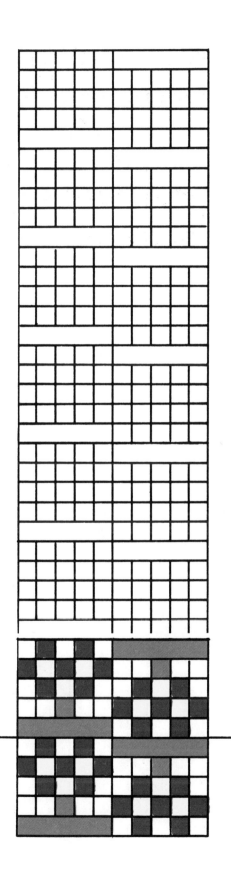

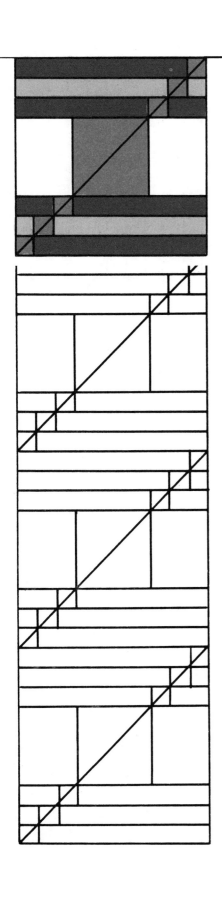

Design No. 79

Border Size   20   inches in width
Pattern Repeat   20   inches
Quilt Size   Queen
Number of Repeats for entire Quilt   14
Frame Measurements:
  Side Panels: 2   inches by   124   inches
  Top and Bottom Panels: 2   inches by   104   inches
Corner Measurements: 20   inches square

Color	Number of templates in repeat	Number of templates in total border	Template code
White	2	28	R96
Green	12	168	T3
	2	28	T28
Gold	2	28	S3
	2	28	R34
Henna	2	28	R25
	2	28	R33
	2	28	R35
Total	**26**	**364**	

Design No. 80

Border Size 20 inches in width
Pattern Repeat 20 inches
Quilt Size Queen
Number of Repeats for entire Quilt 14
Frame Measurements:
  Side Panels: 2 inches by 124 inches
  Top and Bottom Panels: 2 inches by 104 inches
Corner Measurements: 20 inches square

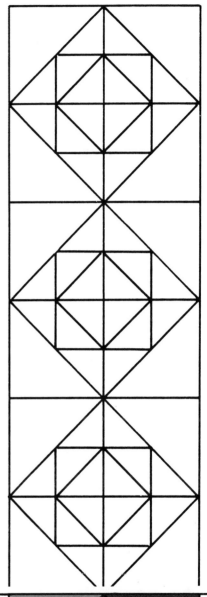

Color	Number of templates in repeat	Number of templates in total border	Template code
Light Purple	4	56	T19
White	2	28	T19
Pumpkin	2	28	T19
	2	28	T32
Dark Purple	8	112	T19
	2	28	T32
Total	**20**	**280**	

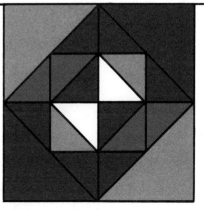

6
Designing Your Own

If you have chosen to color the grids in the book in a completely new way—you have just designed your own unique quilt! But now, you need to develop your own template charts to determine which size templates you need to cut from each of the fabrics you will use.

The first thing you have to do is determine which size quilt you are going to make—full, queen or king. Since each grid is composed of 6 squares across and 8 squares down, the size of the quilt depends upon the measurement of these squares. As we mentioned before in the construction chapter, in order to make a full-sized quilt, you need to use a 9-inch square, for a queen a 10-inch square, and for a king a 12-inch square. See the following illustration of how the squares fit into the overall design:

To show you how to figure out the measurements and numbers of the templates in your quilt top, we have taken our design on page 80 and re-colored it, creating a different design.

Let's take an example. We've chosen to make a full-sized quilt from this new design. In order to figure out our template chart, we start with a piece of paper with the following headings:

Color	Template size	Number of templates	Template code

Knowing that we are dealing in 9-inch squares, we can easily figure out the various sized templates within that square. For instance, if we divide the square into 8 triangles, each triangle will measure $4\frac{1}{2}'' \times 4\frac{1}{2}''$. If we divide it into 9 squares, each square will measure $3'' \times 3''$. If we divide it into 6 rectangles, each rectangle will measure $1\frac{1}{2}'' \times 9''$.

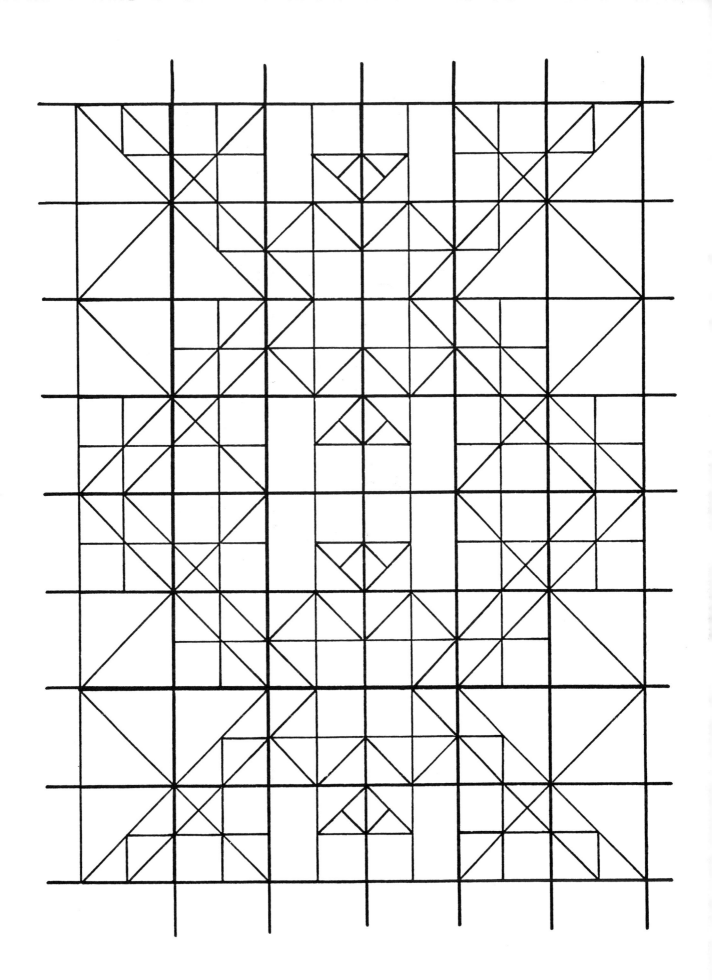

203

Drawing heavy black lines over your design indicating the placement of the 9-inch squares will help you see the different template sizes.

The following grids illustrate how to figure out the template sizes for three different template configurations for each of the three quilt sizes:

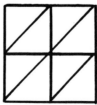   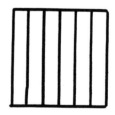

Full	4½″ × 4½″	3″ × 3″	1½″ × 9″
Queen	5″ × 5″	3⅓″ × 3⅓″	1⅔″ × 10″
King	6″ × 6″	4″ × 4″	2″ × 12″

It is easiest to start with one color at a time, so let's start with the color blue. Looking at the grid, we see that there are three different shapes of blue templates: square, triangle and rectangle. Starting with the squares, we see that all of the squares are the same size (¼ of a 9-inch square). This means that each blue square in this quilt will measure 4½″ × 4½″ when pieced into the quilt top. Referring to the template chart on page 213, we see that this size template is template code S13. If we count the number of blue squares in the total quilt top, we find that there are 12. See the following illustration which shows the location of the 12 squares. (You may find it helpful to have two photocopies of the grid to work with—one to use in designing the top and the other to mark and color as you develop your template chart.)

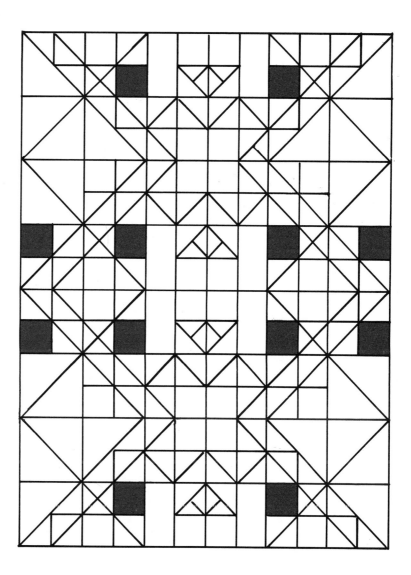

Fill in this information on your sheet like this:

Color	Template size	Number of templates	Template code
Blue	4½″ × 4½″	12	S13

The next template shape is a triangle. There are two sizes of triangles in this design so let's start with the smaller one, which is one quarter of a 4½ inch square. Looking at the template chart on page 238, we see that the template code is T8. If we count the number of these smaller triangles, we find that there are 8. Fill in the chart with this information.

The larger triangle, which is half of a 4½ inch square, measures 4½" × 4½". The template code for this size is T15. Counting these triangles, we find that there are 48 in the quilt top. Fill in this information.

The last shape is a rectangle. Looking at the grid, we see that the rectangle is ½ of a 9-inch square. Therefore, it measures 4½" × 9". Looking up this size on page 218, we see that the template code is R83. Counting, we find that there are 8 of these templates in the quilt top. Fill in this information.

By now your chart should look like this:

Color	Template size	Number of templates	Template code
Blue	4½" × 4½"	12	S13
	3³⁄₁₆" × 3³⁄₁₆"	8	T8
	4½" × 4½"	48	T15
	4½" × 9"	8	R83

If we add the templates together, there should be 76 blue templates in the quilt top. Now, count the blue templates, regardless of their size and shape. Do you count 76? Good! That's a good check along the way to make sure that you don't make mistakes.

Follow the same procedure for the colors salmon and white. If your chart matches the one following, you have the idea. If it doesn't, re-check your numbers.

You must be accurate when developing your template chart. If you make a mistake on your chart, your yardage calculations may be wrong and you may not buy enough fabric of a particular color—which will be a problem if the store runs out of that fabric before you discover your mistake!

Color	Template size	Number of templates	Template code
Blue	4½" × 4½"	12	S13
	3³⁄₁₆" × 3³⁄₁₆"	8	T8
	4½" × 4½"	48	T15
	4½" × 9"	8	R83
Salmon	4½" × 4½"	8	S13
	4½" × 4½"	56	T15
	3³⁄₁₆" × 3³⁄₁₆"	32	T8
White	4½" × 4½"	20	S13
	3³⁄₁₆" × 3³⁄₁₆"	8	T8
	4½" × 4½"	48	T15
	9" × 9"	24	T31
	Total	272	

Another quick check is to compare your total number of templates with ours. If they match, you are fine. If not, you have miss-counted. Also, compare your template codes with the ones on our chart. You should have the same codes as ours as well as the same total templates for each regardless of the color.

You can follow the same procedure for the borders, keeping in mind that the border measurements also change for each quilt size. Each border is marked with the quilt size, length of the pattern repeat, width of the border and number of repeats for the entire quilt. Again, your totals should match ours and your template codes should be the same.

7
Templates

Of all the steps involved in making a quilt, making accurate template patterns is perhaps the most important in ensuring that the finished quilt will look like your original design. Because making a patchwork quilt means sewing many small pieces of fabric together to make a design, the template patterns which you use to trace and cut the fabric templates must be precisely made. Spending the time necessary to get the template measurements perfect will save you hours of frustration while you are piecing your quilt.

To make your template patterns, you will need the following supplies:

8 lines to the inch graph paper
rubber cement
24-inch ruler
razor blade knife (or single-edged razor blade)
sharp pencil or marker
stiff cardboard

To begin, write down the size of the templates you need to make your quilt. Simply look up the template code given on the page on which the quilt top is shown and refer to the template code chart in the yardage charts chapter beginning on page 210 to see what size the template code measures. Do the same for the border templates.

You need one template pattern for each different size piece of fabric in your design. Because the template measurements are given for the size of the piece as it will be in the finished quilt, *you will have to add a seam allowance* to each side before using the pattern to trace and cut the pieces from the fabric. Using 8 lines to the inch graph paper makes this easy. Most graph paper is sold in 8½ inch by 11 inch sheets, so if your template will be larger than this, tape several sheets together until you reach the required size. When you do this, be certain that you line up the graph paper perfectly so that the inch designations match.

Since each square equals ⅛ inch, you can use the graph squares rather than the markings on the ruler as a guide.

The template measurements given in this book reflect only two sides of each template. The dotted lines on the illustrations below show you which measurements are given:

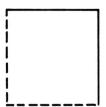 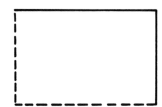 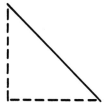

With your ruler, draw a line on the graph paper equal to one side of the template. After this line has been drawn, put your ruler perpendicular to the line at one end and draw the other measurement. To complete the first pattern, connect the lines you have just drawn to create the shape you need, whether a square, rectangle or triangle. This template should now match in width and length, the size of the piece *after* sewing.

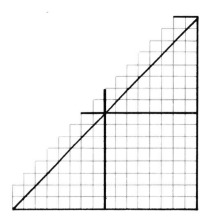

To add the ⅜ inch seam allowance, simply count three squares outside the first two lines you drew and draw lines parallel to these lines. To complete the final template pattern, connect these new lines around the template. You should now have a template that measures ⁶⁄₈ inches more in width and length than the original measurements. For instance, if you began by drawing template code S3 (a square template measuring 3″ × 3″ when pieced), you should now have a template that measures 3⁶⁄₈″ × 3⁶⁄₈″.

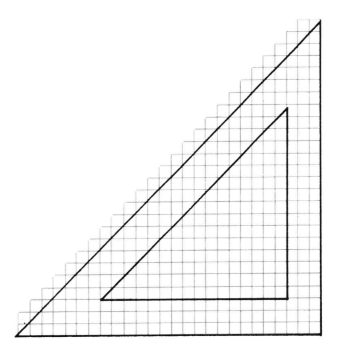

Before we go to the next step, take your ruler and measure the template you've just drawn. If it is the precise shape you need, continue—if not, re-draw the template.

Since you will be tracing around the template several times, you will need to stiffen it so that it will retain its shape. One way to do this is to glue the graph paper to a sheet of stiff cardboard with rubber cement. Do this next, making sure that the graph paper is firmly affixed. Now, take your ruler and place it along the inside of the template pattern, almost touching the line on one side. Take your razor blade and cut this side of the template, using the ruler as a guide. Continue cutting along each side until your template pattern is complete.

Measure the template once again to make sure it is the correct size.

The final test is to see if, by using the template, your fabric can be cut to the right size. So take a piece of the fabric and using the marker that you will use to trace all of the pieces, mark the fabric for cutting. Cut the fabric around the outline and measure the fabric piece. If it is correct—you've done it!

8
Yardage Charts

The yardage charts which follow are designed to eliminate fabric waste, so that regardless of whether you are making a quilt from a design colored as shown in this book, or one which you have colored differently, you will buy the exact amount of fabric which you will need.

There are three different charts: one each for square, rectangular, and triangular templates. Before each chart, we have given you the measurements of the templates (without the seam allowances) along with the template codes. It is always a good idea to check the size of your template with the appropriate code before looking up the yardage required.

Remember that the way in which you arrange the templates on the fabric will affect the number of pieces you can cut from the fabric. Here are some tips to follow:

Square Templates: Square templates are traced in rows with ¼ inch between each template.

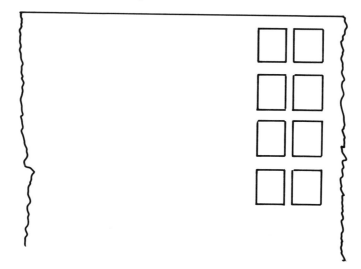

Triangular Templates: In order to get the maximum number of pieces from each yard of fabric, triangular templates are traced with the first row right side up and the second row reversed. Unless you are using an equilaterial triangle (two sides being equal in length), the template has a right and wrong side, so be sure to keep the same side of the template up.

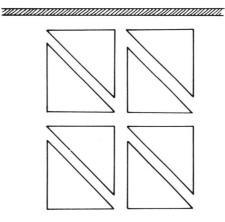

Rectangular Templates: Depending on the size of the template, the width of the fabric, and the number of yards of the fabric, rectangular templates should be traced with either the short side along the selvage or the long side along the selvage. The yardage charts for rectangles contain an "*" sign next to the number when the templates should be placed with the long side along the selvage. The numbers without this sign mean that the short side of the rectangle should be placed along the selvage as illustrated below:

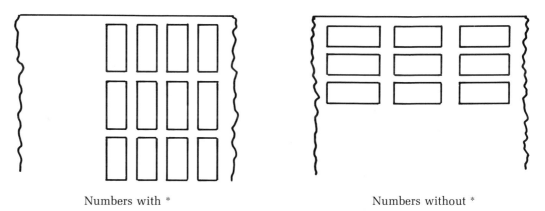

Numbers with *   Numbers without *

Using the yardage charts

To use the yardage charts in this book, simply look up the number of templates you will need for each color and template in your quilt and go to the left side of the chart where you will find the required yardage. Each chart gives the yardage for 36-inch wide and 45-inch wide fabric. It is a good idea to write down both yardage requirements before you go to the fabric store, so that you will know exactly how much to buy regardless of fabric width.

For example, let's say that we need 78 templates of template code R14. We would look at the chart until we found template code R14 on the top. We then scan down the row until we come to the number 78. But there is

211

36 " WIDE FABRIC

TEMPLATE CODES

YARDS	R9	R10	R11	R12	R13	R14	R15	R16
0.25	6	6	3	26*	18	13*	9	9
0.50	14	14	7	52*	39*	26*	18	18
0.75	20	20	14*	80	60	40	30	30
1.00	28	28	14	104	78	52	39	39
1.25	36	36	28*	130*	96	65*	52*	52*
(1.50)	42	42	28*	160	120	(91*)	65*	60
1.75	50	50	42*	184	138	104*	78*	69
2.00	56	56	42*	208	156	117*	91*	78
2.25	70*	64	56*	240	180	130*	104*	91*
2.50	72	72	56*	264	198	143*	117*	104*
2.75	84*	78	70*	296	222	156*	130*	117*
3.00	86	86	70*	320	240	182*	143*	120
3.25	98*	92	84*	344	258	195*	156*	130*
3.50	100	100	84*	377*	282	208*	169*	143*
3.75	112*	108	98*	403*	300	221*	182*	156*
4.00	126*	114	98*	429*	318	234*	195*	169*
4.25	126*	122	112*	456	342	247*	208*	171
4.50	140*	128	112*	481*	360	273*	221*	182*
4.75	140*	136	126*	512	384	286*	234*	195*
5.00	154*	144	126*	536	402	299*	247*	208*

45 " WIDE FABRIC

TEMPLATE CODES

YARDS	R9	R10	R11	R12	R13	R14	R15	R16
0.25	6	6	6	32*	21	16*	12	12
0.50	18*	18*	14	64*	48*	32*	24	24
0.75	20	20	20	100	70	50	40	40
1.00	36*	36*	28	130	96*	65	52	52
(1.25)	36	36	36	160	112	(80)	64	64
1.50	54*	54*	42	200	144*	112*	80	80
1.75	54*	54*	54*	230	161	128*	96*	92
2.00	72*	72*	56	260	192*	144*	112*	104
2.25	90*	72*	72*	300	210	160*	128*	120
2.50	90*	90*	72	330	240*	176*	144*	132
2.75	108*	90*	90*	370	259	192*	160*	148
3.00	108*	108*	90*	400	288*	224*	176*	160
3.25	126*	108*	108*	430	304*	240*	192*	172
3.50	126*	126*	108*	470	336*	256*	208*	188
3.75	144*	126*	126*	500	352*	272*	224*	200
4.00	162*	144*	126*	530	384*	288*	240*	212
4.25	162*	144*	144*	570	400*	304*	256*	228
4.50	180*	162*	144*	600	432*	336*	272*	240
4.75	180*	162*	162*	640	448	352*	288*	256
5.00	198*	180*	162*	670	480*	368*	304*	268

no 78 on the chart. The nearest numbers are 91 and 65, so we take the higher number and look to the left. Now we see that in order to make 78 templates of template code R14, we need to buy 1.5 yards of fabric if the fabric width is 36 inches. Looking at the chart for the 45-inch wide fabric, we see that we would need to purchase only 1.25 yards.

Square Template Codes and Measurements

Code	Measurement without seam allowance
S1	1½″ × 1½″
S2	1⅔″ × 1⅔″
S3	2″ × 2″
S4	2⅛″ × 2½″
S5	2¼″ × 2¼″
S6	2¾″ × 2¾″
S7	3″ × 3″
S8	3³⁄₁₆″ × 3³⁄₁₆″
S9	3⅓″ × 3⅓″
S10	3½″ × 3½″
S11	4″ × 4″
S12	4¼″ × 4¼″
S13	4½″ × 4½″
S14	4¾″ × 4¾″
S15	5″ × 5″
S16	5⅝″ × 5⅝″
S17	6″ × 6″
S18	6⅜″ × 6⅜″
S19	6⅔″ × 6⅔″
S20	7″ × 7″
S21	7½″ × 7½″
S22	8″ × 8″
S23	8½″ × 8½″
S24	9″ × 9″
S25	10″ × 10″
S26	12″ × 12″
S27	2½″ × 2½″
S28	8⅓″ × 8⅓″

36 " WIDE FABRIC

TEMPLATE CODES

YARDS	S1	S2	S3	S4	S5	S6	S7	S8
0.25	42	39	36	22	22	18	18	16
0.50	98	78	72	55	55	36	36	32
0.75	140	130	108	88	88	63	54	48
1.00	196	169	144	121	121	81	81	64
1.25	252	208	180	154	143	108	99	80
1.50	294	260	216	187	176	126	117	96
1.75	350	299	252	220	209	144	135	120
2.00	392	338	288	253	242	171	162	136
2.25	448	390	324	275	264	189	180	152
2.50	504	429	360	308	297	216	198	168
2.75	546	481	396	341	330	234	216	184
3.00	602	520	432	374	363	252	243	200
3.25	644	559	468	407	396	279	261	216
3.50	700	611	504	440	418	297	279	240
3.75	756	650	540	473	451	324	297	256
4.00	798	689	576	506	484	342	324	272
4.25	854	741	612	528	517	360	342	288
4.50	896	780	648	561	539	387	360	304
4.75	952	832	684	594	572	405	378	320
5.00	1008	871	720	627	605	432	405	336

45 " WIDE FABRIC

TEMPLATE CODES

YARDS	S1	S2	S3	S4	S5	S6	S7	S8
0.25	54	48	45	28	26	24	22	20
0.50	126	96	90	70	65	48	44	40
0.75	180	160	135	112	104	84	66	60
1.00	252	208	180	154	143	108	99	80
1.25	324	256	225	196	169	144	121	100
1.50	378	320	270	238	208	168	143	120
1.75	450	368	315	280	247	192	165	150
2.00	504	416	360	322	286	228	198	170
2.25	576	480	405	350	312	252	220	190
2.50	648	528	450	392	351	288	242	210
2.75	702	592	495	434	390	312	264	230
3.00	774	640	540	476	429	336	297	250
3.25	828	688	585	518	468	372	319	270
3.50	900	752	630	560	494	396	341	300
3.75	972	800	675	602	533	432	363	320
4.00	1026	848	720	644	572	456	396	340
4.25	1098	912	765	672	611	480	418	360
4.50	1152	960	810	714	637	516	440	380
4.75	1224	1024	855	756	676	540	462	400
5.00	1296	1072	900	798	715	576	495	420

36 " WIDE FABRIC

TEMPLATE CODES

YARDS	S9	S10	S11	S12	S13	S14	S15	S16
0.25	16	16	7	6	6	6	6	5
0.50	32	32	21	18	18	18	18	10
0.75	48	48	35	30	24	24	24	20
1.00	64	64	49	36	36	36	36	25
1.25	80	80	63	48	48	42	42	30
1.50	96	96	70	60	54	54	54	40
1.75	112	112	84	72	66	60	60	45
2.00	128	128	98	78	78	72	72	50
2.25	144	144	112	90	84	84	78	60
2.50	160	160	126	102	96	90	90	65
2.75	176	176	133	108	108	102	96	70
3.00	192	192	147	120	114	108	108	80
3.25	208	208	161	132	126	120	114	85
3.50	232	224	175	144	132	126	126	95
3.75	248	240	189	150	144	138	132	100
4.00	264	256	196	162	156	150	144	105
4.25	280	272	210	174	162	156	150	115
4.50	296	288	224	180	174	168	162	120
4.75	312	304	238	192	186	174	168	125
5.00	328	320	252	204	192	186	180	135

45 " WIDE FABRIC

TEMPLATE CODES

YARDS	S9	S10	S11	S12	S13	S14	S15	S16
0.25	20	20	9	8	8	7	7	6
0.50	40	40	27	24	24	21	21	12
0.75	60	60	45	40	32	28	28	24
1.00	80	80	63	48	48	42	42	30
1.25	100	100	81	64	64	49	49	36
1.50	120	120	90	80	72	63	63	48
1.75	140	140	108	96	88	70	70	54
2.00	160	160	126	104	104	84	84	60
2.25	180	180	144	120	112	98	91	72
2.50	200	200	162	136	128	105	105	78
2.75	220	220	171	144	144	119	112	84
3.00	240	240	189	160	152	126	126	96
3.25	260	260	207	176	168	140	133	102
3.50	290	280	225	192	176	147	147	114
3.75	310	300	243	200	192	161	154	120
4.00	330	320	252	216	208	175	168	126
4.25	350	340	270	232	216	182	175	138
4.50	370	360	288	240	232	196	189	144
4.75	390	380	306	256	248	203	196	150
5.00	410	400	324	272	256	217	210	162

36 " WIDE FABRIC

	TEMPLATE CODES					
YARDS	S17	S18	S19	S20	S21	S22
0.25	5	4	4	4	4	4
0.50	10	8	8	8	8	8
0.75	15	12	12	12	12	12
1.00	25	16	16	16	16	16
1.25	30	24	20	20	20	20
1.50	35	28	28	24	24	24
1.75	45	32	32	28	28	28
2.00	50	36	36	36	32	32
2.25	55	40	40	40	36	36
2.50	60	48	44	44	40	40
2.75	70	52	48	48	44	44
3.00	75	56	56	52	48	48
3.25	80	60	60	56	52	52
3.50	90	68	64	60	56	56
3.75	95	72	68	64	60	60
4.00	100	76	72	72	64	64
4.25	105	80	76	76	72	68
4.50	115	84	84	80	76	72
4.75	120	92	88	84	80	76
5.00	125	96	92	88	84	80

45 " WIDE FABRIC

	TEMPLATE CODES					
YARDS	S17	S18	S19	S20	S21	S22
0.25	6	6	5	5	5	5
0.50	12	12	10	10	10	10
0.75	18	18	15	15	15	15
1.00	30	24	20	20	20	20
1.25	36	36	25	25	25	25
1.50	42	42	35	30	30	30
1.75	54	48	40	35	35	35
2.00	60	54	45	45	40	40
2.25	66	60	50	50	45	45
2.50	72	72	55	55	50	50
2.75	84	78	60	60	55	55
3.00	90	84	70	65	60	60
3.25	96	90	75	70	65	65
3.50	108	102	80	75	70	70
3.75	114	108	85	80	75	75
4.00	120	114	90	90	80	80
4.25	126	120	95	95	90	85
4.50	138	126	105	100	95	90
4.75	144	138	110	105	100	95
5.00	150	144	115	110	105	100

36 " WIDE FABRIC

YARDS	S23	S24	S25	S26	S27	S28
0.25	0	0	0	0	20	0
0.50	3	3	3	2	50	3
0.75	6	6	6	4	70	6
1.00	9	9	9	4	100	9
1.25	12	12	12	6	120	12
1.50	15	15	12	8	150	15
1.75	18	18	15	8	180	18
2.00	21	21	18	10	200	21
2.25	24	24	21	12	230	24
2.50	27	27	24	12	250	27
2.75	30	27	27	14	280	30
3.00	33	30	27	16	300	33
3.25	36	33	30	18	330	36
3.50	39	36	33	18	360	39
3.75	42	39	36	20	380	42
4.00	45	42	39	22	410	45
4.25	48	45	39	22	430	48
4.50	51	48	42	24	460	51
4.75	54	51	45	26	480	54
5.00	54	54	48	26	510	57

45 " WIDE FABRIC

YARDS	S23	S24	S25	S26	S27	S28
0.25	0	0	0	0	24	0
0.50	4	4	4	3	60	4
0.75	8	8	8	6	84	8
1.00	12	12	12	6	120	12
1.25	16	16	16	9	144	16
1.50	20	20	16	12	180	20
1.75	24	24	20	12	216	24
2.00	28	28	24	15	240	28
2.25	32	32	28	18	276	32
2.50	36	36	32	18	300	36
2.75	40	36	36	21	336	40
3.00	44	40	36	24	360	44
3.25	48	44	40	27	396	48
3.50	52	48	44	27	432	52
3.75	56	52	48	30	456	56
4.00	60	56	52	33	492	60
4.25	64	60	52	33	516	64
4.50	68	64	56	36	552	68
4.75	72	68	60	39	576	72
5.00	72	72	64	39	612	76

Rectangle Template Codes and Measurements

Code	Measurement without seam allowance
R1	1½″ × 3″
R2	1½″ × 4½″
R3	1½″ × 6″
R4	1½″ × 7½″
R5	1½″ × 9″
R6	1½″ × 10½″
R7	1½″ × 12″
R8	1½″ × 13½″
R9	1½″ × 15″
R10	1½″ × 16½″
R11	1½″ × 18″
R12	1⅔″ × 3⅓″
R13	1⅔″ × 5″
R14	1⅔″ × 6⅔″
R15	1⅔″ × 8⅓″
R16	1⅔″ × 10″
R17	1⅔″ × 11⅔″
R18	1⅔″ × 13⅓″
R19	1⅔″ × 14″
R20	1⅔″ × 15″
R21	1⅔″ × 16⅔″
R22	1⅔″ × 18⅓″
R23	1⅔″ × 20″
R24	2″ × 3″
R25	2″ × 4″
R26	2″ × 5″
R27	2″ × 6″
R28	2″ × 7″
R29	2″ × 8″
R30	2″ × 9″
R31	2″ × 10″
R32	2″ × 12″
R33	2″ × 14″
R34	2″ × 16″
R35	2″ × 18″
R36	2″ × 20″
R37	2″ × 22″
R38	2″ × 24″
R39	2¼″ × 4½″
R40	2¼″ × 6″
R41	2¼″ × 9″
R42	2¼″ × 13½″
R43	2¼″ × 18″
R44	2½″ × 5″
R45	2½″ × 6⅔″
R46	2½″ × 10″
R47	2½″ × 15″
R48	2½″ × 20″
R49	3″ × 4½″
R50	3″ × 6″
R51	3″ × 7½″
R52	3″ × 8″
R53	3″ × 9″
R54	3″ × 10½″
R55	3″ × 12″
R56	3″ × 13½″
R57	3″ × 15″
R58	3″ × 16½″
R59	3″ × 18″
R60	3″ × 24″

Rectangle Template Codes and Measurements

Code	Measurement without seam allowance
R61	3⅓″ × 5″
R62	3⅓″ × 6⅔″
R63	3⅓″ × 8⅓″
R64	3⅓″ × 10″
R65	3⅓″ × 11⅔″
R66	3⅓″ × 13⅓″
R67	3⅓″ × 15″
R68	3⅓″ × 16⅔″
R69	3⅓″ × 18⅓″
R70	3⅓″ × 20″
R71	4″ × 6″
R72	4″ × 8″
R73	4″ × 10″
R74	4″ × 12″
R75	4″ × 14″
R76	4″ × 16″
R77	4″ × 18″
R78	4″ × 20″
R79	4″ × 22″
R80	4″ × 24″
R81	4½″ × 6″
R82	4½″ × 7½″
R83	4½″ × 9″
R84	4½″ × 13½″
R85	4½″ × 15″
R86	4½″ × 16½″
R87	4½″ × 18″
R88	5″ × 6⅔″
R89	5″ × 8⅓″
R90	5″ × 10″
R91	5″ × 15″
R92	5″ × 16⅔″
R93	5″ × 18⅓″
R94	5″ × 20″
R95	6″ × 7½″
R96	6″ × 8″
R97	6″ × 9″
R98	6″ × 10″
R99	6″ × 10½″
R100	6″ × 12″
R101	6″ × 15″
R102	6″ × 18″
R103	6″ × 20″
R104	6″ × 22″
R105	6″ × 24″
R106	6⅔″ × 8⅓″
R107	6⅔″ × 10″
R108	6⅔″ × 11⅔″
R109	6⅔″ × 13⅓″
R110	6⅔″ × 16⅔″
R111	6⅔″ × 20″
R112	7½″ × 9″
R113	7½″ × 10½″
R114	8″ × 10″
R115	8″ × 12″
R116	8″ × 14″
R117	8″ × 16″
R118	8″ × 20″
R119	8″ × 24″
R120	8⅓″ × 10″

Rectangle Template Codes and Measurements

Code	Measurement without seam allowance
R121	8⅓″ × 11⅔″
R122	9″ × 12″
R123	9″ × 16½″
R124	9″ × 18″
R125	10″ × 12″
R126	10″ × 13⅓″
R127	10″ × 14″
R128	10″ × 18⅓″
R129	10″ × 20″
R130	10½″ × 15″
R131	10½″ × 18″

Rectangle Template Codes and Measurements

Code	Measurement without seam allowance
R132	11⅔″ × 16⅔″
R133	11⅔″ × 20″
R134	12″ × 16″
R135	12″ × 18″
R136	12″ × 22″
R137	12″ × 24″
R138	13⅓″ × 20″
R139	14″ × 20″
R140	14″ × 24″
R141	16″ × 24″

36 " WIDE FABRIC

TEMPLATE CODES

YARDS	R1	R2	R3	R4	R5	R6	R7	R8
0.25	28*	18	15	14*	9	9	6	6
0.50	63	42	35	28	21	21	14	14
0.75	90	60	50	42*	30	30	28*	20
1.00	126	84	70	56	42	42	28	28
1.25	162	112*	90	72	56*	54	42*	42*
1.50	189	126	105	84	70*	63	56*	42
1.75	225	154*	126*	100	84*	75	56*	56*
2.00	252	182*	140	112	98*	84	70*	56
2.25	288	196*	160	128	112*	98*	84*	70*
2.50	324	224*	180	144	126*	108	84*	84*
2.75	351	252*	196*	156	126*	117	98*	84*
3.00	387	266*	215	172	140*	129	112*	98*
3.25	414	294*	230	184	154*	140*	126*	112*
3.50	450	308*	252*	200	168*	150	126*	112*
3.75	486	336*	270	216	182*	162	140*	126*
4.00	513	364*	285	228	196*	171	154*	126*
4.25	549	378*	305	252*	210*	183	154*	140*
4.50	576	406*	322*	266*	224*	196*	168*	154*
4.75	612	434*	340	280*	238*	204	182*	154*
5.00	648	448*	360	294*	252*	216	182*	168*

45 " WIDE FABRIC

TEMPLATE CODES

YARDS	R1	R2	R3	R4	R5	R6	R7	R8
0.25	36*	24	18	18*	12	9	9	9
0.50	77	56	42	36*	28	21	21	21
0.75	110	80	60	54*	40	36*	36*	30
1.00	162*	112	90*	72*	56	54*	42	42
1.25	198	144	108	90	72	54	54	54
1.50	234*	168	126	108*	90*	72*	72*	63
1.75	275	200	162*	126*	108*	90*	75	75
2.00	324*	234*	180*	144*	126	108*	90*	84
2.25	360*	256	198*	162*	144*	126*	108*	96
2.50	396	288	216	180	162*	126*	108	108
2.75	432*	324*	252*	198*	162*	144*	126*	117
3.00	486*	344	270*	216*	180*	162*	144*	129
3.25	522*	378*	288*	234*	198*	180*	162*	144*
3.50	558*	400	324*	252*	216*	180*	162*	150
3.75	594	432	342*	270	234*	198*	180*	162
4.00	648*	468*	360*	288*	252*	216*	198*	171
4.25	684*	488	378*	324*	270*	234*	198*	183
4.50	720*	522*	414*	342*	288*	252*	216*	198*
4.75	756*	558*	432*	360*	306*	252*	234*	204
5.00	810*	576	450*	378*	324*	270*	234*	216

36 " WIDE FABRIC

TEMPLATE CODES

YARDS	R9	R10	R11	R12	R13	R14	R15	R16
0.25	6	6	3	26*	18	13*	9	9
0.50	14	14	7	52*	39*	26*	18	18
0.75	20	20	14*	80	60	40	30	30
1.00	28	28	14	104	78	52	39	39
1.25	36	36	28*	130*	96	65*	52*	52*
1.50	42	42	28*	160	120	91*	65*	60
1.75	50	50	42*	184	138	104*	78*	69
2.00	56	56	42*	208	156	117*	91*	78
2.25	70*	64	56*	240	180	130*	104*	91*
2.50	72	72	56*	264	198	143*	117*	104*
2.75	84*	78	70*	296	222	156*	130*	117*
3.00	86	86	70*	320	240	182*	143*	120
3.25	98*	92	84*	344	258	195*	156*	130*
3.50	100	100	84*	377*	282	208*	169*	143*
3.75	112*	108	98*	403*	300	221*	182*	156*
4.00	126*	114	98*	429*	318	234*	195*	169*
4.25	126*	122	112*	456	342	247*	208*	171
4.50	140*	128	112*	481*	360	273*	221*	182*
4.75	140*	136	126*	512	384	286*	234*	195*
5.00	154*	144	126*	536	402	299*	247*	208*

45 " WIDE FABRIC

TEMPLATE CODES

YARDS	R9	R10	R11	R12	R13	R14	R15	R16
0.25	6	6	6	32*	21	16*	12	12
0.50	18*	18*	14	64*	48*	32*	24	24
0.75	20	20	20	100	70	50	40	40
1.00	36*	36*	28	130	96*	65	52	52
1.25	36	36	36	160	112	80	64	64
1.50	54*	54*	42	200	144*	112*	80	80
1.75	54*	54*	54*	230	161	128*	96*	92
2.00	72*	72*	56	260	192*	144*	112*	104
2.25	90*	72*	72*	300	210	160*	128*	120
2.50	90*	90*	72	330	240*	176*	144*	132
2.75	108*	90*	90*	370	259	192*	160*	148
3.00	108*	108*	90*	400	288*	224*	176*	160
3.25	126*	108*	108*	430	304*	240*	192*	172
3.50	126*	126*	108*	470	336*	256*	208*	188
3.75	144*	126*	126*	500	352*	272*	224*	200
4.00	162*	144*	126*	530	384*	288*	240*	212
4.25	162*	144*	144*	570	400*	304*	256*	228
4.50	180*	162*	144*	600	432*	336*	272*	240
4.75	180*	162*	162*	640	448	352*	288*	256
5.00	198*	180*	162*	670	480*	368*	304*	268

36 " WIDE FABRIC

TEMPLATE CODES

YARDS	R17	R18	R19	R20	R21	R22	R23	R24
0.25	6	6	6	6	6	3	3	27
0.50	13*	13*	13*	13*	13*	6	6	54
0.75	26*	20	20	20	20	13*	13*	81
1.00	26	26	26	26	26	13	13	108
1.25	39*	39*	39*	32	32	26*	26*	135
1.50	52*	40	40	40	40	26*	26*	162
1.75	52*	52*	52*	46	46	39*	39*	189
2.00	65*	65*	52	52	52	39*	39*	216
2.25	78*	65*	65*	65*	60	52*	39*	243
2.50	91*	78*	78*	66	66	52*	52*	270
2.75	91*	78*	78*	78*	74	65*	52*	297
3.00	104*	91*	91*	80	80	65*	65*	324
3.25	117*	104*	91*	91*	86	78*	65*	351
3.50	117*	104*	104*	94	94	78*	78*	378
3.75	130*	117*	117*	104*	100	78*	78*	405
4.00	143*	130*	117*	117*	106	91*	78*	432
4.25	156*	130*	130*	117*	114	91*	91*	459
4.50	156*	143*	130*	130*	120	104*	91*	486
4.75	169*	143*	143*	130*	128	104*	104*	513
5.00	182*	156*	156*	143*	134	117*	104*	540

45 " WIDE FABRIC

TEMPLATE CODES

YARDS	R17	R18	R19	R20	R21	R22	R23	R24
0.25	9	9	9	6	6	6	6	33
0.50	18	18	18	16*	16*	12	12	66
0.75	32*	30	30	20	20	20	20	99
1.00	39	39	39	32*	32*	26	26	135*
1.25	48	48	48	32	32	32	32	165
1.50	64*	60	60	48*	48*	40	40	198
1.75	69	69	69	48*	48*	48*	48*	231
2.00	80*	80*	78	64*	64*	52	52	270*
2.25	96*	90	90	80*	64*	64*	60	300*
2.50	112*	99	99	80*	80*	66	66	330
2.75	112*	111	111	96*	80*	80*	74	363
3.00	128*	120	120	96*	96*	80	80	405*
3.25	144*	129	129	112*	96*	96*	86	435*
3.50	144*	141	141	112*	112*	96*	96*	465*
3.75	160*	150	150	128*	112*	100	100	495
4.00	176*	160*	159	144*	128*	112*	106	540*
4.25	192*	171	171	144*	128*	114	114	570*
4.50	192*	180	180	160*	144*	128*	120	600*
4.75	208*	192	192	160*	144*	128	128	630*
5.00	224*	201	201	176*	160*	144*	134	675*

36 " WIDE FABRIC

TEMPLATE CODES

YARDS	R25	R26	R27	R28	R29	R30	R31	R32
0.25	21	18	15	12	12	9	9	6
0.50	42	36	30	24	24	18	18	12
0.75	63	54	45	36	36	27	27	24*
1.00	84	72	60	48	48	36	36	24
1.25	108*	90	75	60	60	48*	48*	36*
1.50	126	108	90	72	72	60*	54	48*
1.75	147	126	108*	84	84	72*	63	48*
2.00	168	144	120	108*	96	84*	72	60*
2.25	192*	162	135	120*	108	96*	84*	72*
2.50	216*	180	150	132*	120	108*	96*	72*
2.75	231	198	168*	144*	132	108*	108*	84*
3.00	252	216	180	156*	144	120*	108	96*
3.25	276*	234	195	168*	156	132*	120*	108*
3.50	300*	252	216*	180*	168	144*	132*	108*
3.75	324*	270	228*	192*	180	156*	144*	120*
4.00	336	288	240	216*	192	168*	156*	132*
4.25	360*	306	255	228*	204	180*	156*	132*
4.50	384*	324	276*	240*	216	192*	168*	144*
4.75	408*	342	288*	252*	228	204*	180*	156*
5.00	432*	360	300	264*	240	216*	192*	156*

45 " WIDE FABRIC

TEMPLATE CODES

YARDS	R25	R26	R27	R28	R29	R30	R31	R32
0.25	27	21	18	15	15	12	12	9
0.50	54	45*	36	30	30	24	24	18
0.75	81	63	54	45	45	36	36	30*
1.00	108	90*	75*	60	60	48	48	36
1.25	135	105	90	75	75	60	60	45
1.50	162	135*	108	90	90	75*	72	60*
1.75	189	150*	135*	105	105	90*	84	63
2.00	216	180*	150*	135*	120	105*	96	75*
2.25	243	195*	165*	150*	135	120*	108	90*
2.50	270	225*	180	165*	150	135*	120	90
2.75	297	240*	210*	180*	165	135*	135*	105*
3.00	324	270*	225*	195*	180	150*	144	120*
3.25	351	285*	240*	210*	195	165*	156	135*
3.50	378	315*	270*	225*	210	180*	168	135*
3.75	405	330*	285*	240*	225	195*	180	150*
4.00	432	360*	300*	270*	240	210*	195*	165*
4.25	459	375*	315*	285*	255	225*	204	165*
4.50	486	405*	345*	300*	270	240*	216	180*
4.75	513	420*	360*	315*	285	255*	228	195*
5.00	540	450*	375*	330*	300	270*	240	195*

36 " WIDE FABRIC

TEMPLATE CODES

YARDS	R33	R34	R35	R36	R37	R38	R39	R40
0.25	6	6	3	3	3	3	12	11*
0.50	12	12	6	6	6	6	33*	25
0.75	18	18	12*	12*	12*	12*	48	40
1.00	24	24	12	12	12	12	66	55
1.25	36*	30	24*	24*	15	15	88*	66*
1.50	36	36	24*	24*	24*	24*	99*	80
1.75	48*	42	36*	36*	24*	24*	121*	99*
2.00	48	48	36*	36*	36*	24	143*	110
2.25	60*	54	48*	36*	36*	36*	154*	121*
2.50	72*	60	48*	48*	36*	36*	176*	135
2.75	72*	66	60*	48*	48*	36*	198*	154*
3.00	84*	72	60*	60*	48*	48*	209*	165
3.25	84*	78	72*	60*	60*	48*	231*	180
3.50	96*	84	72*	72*	60*	60*	242*	198*
3.75	108*	90	84*	72*	60*	60*	264*	209*
4.00	108*	96	84*	72*	72*	60*	286*	220
4.25	120*	108*	96*	84*	72*	72*	297*	235
4.50	120*	108	96*	84*	84*	72*	319*	253*
4.75	132*	120*	108*	96*	84*	72*	341*	264*
5.00	144*	120	108*	96*	84*	84*	352*	275

45 " WIDE FABRIC

TEMPLATE CODES

YARDS	R33	R34	R35	R36	R37	R38	R39	R40
0.25	9	6	6	6	3	3	16	13*
0.50	18	15*	12	12	6	6	40	30
0.75	27	18	18	18	15*	15*	64	48
1.00	36	30*	24	24	15*	15*	88	66
1.25	45	30	30	30	15	15	104	78
1.50	54	45*	36	36	30*	30*	128	96
1.75	63	45*	45*	45*	30*	30*	152	117*
2.00	72	60*	48	48	45*	30*	176	132
2.25	81	60*	60*	54	45*	45*	192	144
2.50	90	75*	60	60	45*	45*	216	162
2.75	99	75*	75*	66	60*	45*	240	182*
3.00	108	90*	75*	75*	60*	60*	264	198
3.25	117	90*	90*	78	75*	60*	288	216
3.50	126	105*	90*	90*	75*	75*	304	234*
3.75	135	105*	105*	90	75*	75*	328	247*
4.00	144	120*	105*	96	90*	75*	352	264
4.25	153	135*	120*	105*	90*	90*	376	282
4.50	162	135*	120*	108	105*	90*	392	299*
4.75	171	150*	135*	120*	105*	90*	416	312
5.00	180	150*	135*	120	105*	105*	440	330

36 " WIDE FABRIC

TEMPLATE CODES

YARDS	R41	R42	R43	R44	R45	R46	R47	R48
0.25	6	4	2	12	10*	6	4	2
0.50	15	11*	5	30	20	15	10	5
0.75	24	16	11*	42	30*	21	14	10*
1.00	33	22	11	60	40	30	20	10
1.25	44*	33*	22*	72	50*	40*	24	20*
1.50	55*	33*	22*	90	70*	45	30	20*
1.75	66*	44*	33*	108	80*	54	36	30*
2.00	77*	44	33*	120	90*	60	40	30*
2.25	88*	55*	44*	138	100*	70*	50*	30*
2.50	99*	66*	44*	150	110*	80*	50	40*
2.75	99*	66*	55*	168	120*	90*	60*	40*
3.00	110*	77*	55*	180	140*	90	60	50*
3.25	121*	88*	66*	198	150*	100*	70*	50*
3.50	132*	88*	66*	216	160*	110*	72	60*
3.75	143*	99*	77*	228	170*	120*	80*	60*
4.00	154*	99*	77*	246	180*	130*	90*	60*
4.25	165*	110*	88*	258	190*	130*	90*	70*
4.50	176*	121*	88*	276	210*	140*	100*	70*
4.75	187*	121*	99*	288	220*	150*	100*	80*
5.00	198*	132*	99*	306	230*	160*	110*	80*

45 " WIDE FABRIC

TEMPLATE CODES

YARDS	R41	R42	R43	R44	R45	R46	R47	R48
0.25	8	6	4	14	12*	8	4	4
0.50	20	15	10	36*	25	20	12*	10
0.75	32	24	16	49	36*	28	14	14
1.00	44	33	22	72*	50	40	24*	20
1.25	52	39	26	84	60	48	24	24
1.50	65*	48	32	108*	84*	60	36*	30
1.75	78*	57	39*	126	96*	72	36	36
2.00	91*	66	44	144*	108*	80	48*	40
2.25	104*	72	52*	161	120*	92	60*	46
2.50	117*	81	54	180*	132*	100	60*	50
2.75	120	90	65*	196	144*	112	72*	56
3.00	132	99	66	216*	168*	120	72*	60
3.25	144	108	78*	231	180*	132	84*	66
3.50	156*	114	78*	252	192*	144	84*	72
3.75	169*	123	91*	266	204*	152	96*	76
4.00	182*	132	91*	288*	216*	164	108*	82
4.25	195*	141	104*	301	228*	172	108*	86
4.50	208*	147	104*	324*	252*	184	120*	92
4.75	221*	156	117*	336	264*	192	120*	96
5.00	234*	165	117*	360*	276*	204	132*	102

36 " WIDE FABRIC

TEMPLATE CODES

YARDS	R49	R50	R51	R52	R53	R54	R55	R56
0.25	12	10	9*	9*	6	6	4	4
0.50	27*	20	18*	18*	12	12	9*	9*
0.75	36	30	27*	27*	18	18	18*	12
1.00	54	45	36	36	27	27	18	18
1.25	72*	55	45*	45*	36*	33	27*	27*
1.50	81*	65	54*	54*	45*	39	36*	27*
1.75	99*	81*	63*	63*	54*	45	36*	36*
2.00	117*	90	72	72	63*	54	45*	36
2.25	126*	100	81*	81*	72*	63*	54*	45*
2.50	144*	110	90*	90*	81*	66	54*	54*
2.75	162*	126*	99*	99*	81*	72	63*	54*
3.00	171*	135	108	108	90*	81	72*	63*
3.25	189*	145	117*	117*	99*	90*	81*	72*
3.50	198*	162*	126*	126*	108*	93	81*	72*
3.75	216*	171*	135*	135*	117*	99	90*	81*
4.00	234*	180	144	144	126*	108	99*	81*
4.25	243*	190	162*	153*	135*	117*	99*	90*
4.50	261*	207*	171*	162*	144*	126*	108*	99*
4.75	279*	216*	180*	171*	153*	126	117*	99*
5.00	288*	225	189*	180	162*	135	117*	108*

45 " WIDE FABRIC

TEMPLATE CODES

YARDS	R49	R50	R51	R52	R53	R54	R55	R56
0.25	16	12	11*	11*	8	6	6	6
0.50	33*	24	22*	22*	16	12	12	12
0.75	48	36	33*	33*	24	22*	22*	18
1.00	72	55*	45	45	36	33*	27	27
1.25	88	66	55	55	44	33	33	33
1.50	104	78	66*	66*	55*	44*	44*	39
1.75	121*	99*	77*	77*	66*	55*	45	45
2.00	144	110*	90	90	77*	66*	55*	54
2.25	160	121*	100	100	88*	77*	66*	60
2.50	176	132	110	110	99*	77*	66	66
2.75	198*	154*	121*	121*	99*	88*	77*	72
3.00	216	165*	135	135	110*	99*	88*	81
3.25	232	176*	145	145	121*	110*	99*	88*
3.50	248	198*	155	155	132*	110*	99*	93
3.75	264	209*	165	165	143*	121*	110*	99
4.00	288	220*	180	180	154*	132*	121*	108
4.25	304	231*	198*	190	165*	143*	121*	114
4.50	320	253*	209*	200	176*	154*	132*	121*
4.75	341*	264*	220*	210	187*	154*	143*	126
5.00	360	275*	231*	225	198*	165*	143*	135

226

36 " WIDE FABRIC

				TEMPLATE CODES				
YARDS	R57	R58	R59	R60	R61	R62	R63	R64
0.25	4	4	2	2	12	8	6	6
0.50	9*	9*	4	4	24	16	12	12
0.75	12	12	9*	9*	36	24	18	18
1.00	18	18	9	9	48	32	24	24
1.25	22	22	18*	11	60	40	32*	32*
1.50	27*	27*	18*	18*	72	56*	40*	36
1.75	30	30	27*	18*	84	64*	48*	42
2.00	36	36	27*	18	96	72*	56*	48
2.25	45*	40	36*	27*	108	80*	64*	56*
2.50	45*	45*	36*	27*	120	88*	72*	64*
2.75	54*	48	45*	27*	132	96*	80*	72*
3.00	54	54	45*	36*	144	112*	88*	72
3.25	63*	58	54*	36*	156	120*	96*	80*
3.50	63*	63*	54*	45*	174	128*	104*	88*
3.75	72*	66	63*	45*	186	136*	112*	96*
4.00	81*	72	63*	45*	198	144*	120*	104*
4.25	81*	76	72*	54*	210	152*	128*	105
4.50	90*	81*	72*	54*	222	168*	136*	112*
4.75	90*	84	81*	54*	234	176*	144*	120*
5.00	99*	90	81*	63*	246	184*	152*	128*

45 " WIDE FABRIC

				TEMPLATE CODES				
YARDS	R57	R58	R59	R60	R61	R62	R63	R64
0.25	4	4	4	2	14	10	8	8
0.50	11*	11*	8	4	30*	20	16	16
0.75	12	12	12	11*	42	30	24	24
1.00	22*	22*	18	11*	60*	40	32	32
1.25	22	22	22	11	70	50	40	40
1.50	33*	33*	26	22*	90*	70*	50*	48
1.75	33*	33*	33*	22*	100*	80*	60*	56
2.00	44*	44*	36	22*	120*	90*	70*	64
2.25	55*	44*	44*	33*	130*	100*	80*	72
2.50	55*	55*	44	33*	150*	110*	90*	80
2.75	66*	55*	55*	33*	160*	120*	100*	90*
3.00	66*	66*	55*	44*	180*	140*	110*	96
3.25	77*	66*	66*	44*	190*	150*	120*	104
3.50	77*	77*	66*	55*	210*	160*	130*	116
3.75	88*	77*	77*	55*	220*	170*	140*	124
4.00	99*	88*	77*	55*	240*	180*	150*	132
4.25	99*	88*	88*	66*	250*	190*	160*	140
4.50	110*	99*	88*	66*	270*	210*	170*	148
4.75	110*	99*	99*	66*	280*	220*	180*	156
5.00	121*	110*	99*	77*	300*	230*	190*	164

36 " WIDE FABRIC

TEMPLATE CODES

YARDS	R65	R66	R67	R68	R69	R70	R71	R72
0.25	4	4	4	4	2	2	7*	7*
0.50	8	8	8	8	4	4	15	14*
0.75	16*	12	12	12	8*	8*	25	21*
1.00	16	16	16	16	8	8	35	28
1.25	24*	24*	20	20	16*	16*	45	36
1.50	32*	24	24	24	16*	16*	50	42*
1.75	32*	32*	28	28	24*	24*	63*	49*
2.00	40*	40*	32	32	24*	24*	70	56
2.25	48*	40*	40*	36	32*	24*	80	64
2.50	56*	48*	40	40	32*	32*	90	72
2.75	56*	48*	48*	44	40*	32*	98*	77*
3.00	64*	56*	48	48	40*	40*	105	84
3.25	72*	64*	56*	52	48*	40*	115	92
3.50	72*	64*	58	58	48*	48*	126*	100
3.75	80*	72*	64*	62	48*	48*	135	108
4.00	88*	80*	72*	66	56*	48*	140	112
4.25	96*	80*	72*	70	56*	56*	150	120
4.50	96*	88*	80*	74	64*	56*	161*	128
4.75	104*	88*	80*	78	64*	64*	170	136
5.00	112*	96*	88*	82	72*	64*	180	144

45 " WIDE FABRIC

TEMPLATE CODES

YARDS	R65	R66	R67	R68	R69	R70	R71	R72
0.25	6	6	4	4	4	4	9*	9*
0.50	12	12	10*	10*	8	8	18	18*
0.75	20*	18	12	12	12	12	30	27*
1.00	24	24	20*	20*	16	16	45*	36*
1.25	30	30	20	20	20	20	54	45
1.50	40*	36	30*	30*	24	24	63*	54*
1.75	42	42	30*	30*	30*	30*	81*	63*
2.00	50*	50*	40*	40*	32	32	90*	72*
2.25	60*	54	50*	40*	40*	36	99*	81*
2.50	70*	60	50*	50*	40	40	108	90
2.75	70*	66	60*	50*	50*	44	126*	99*
3.00	80*	72	60*	60*	50*	50*	135*	108*
3.25	90*	80*	70*	60*	60*	52	144*	117*
3.50	90*	87	70*	70*	60*	60*	162*	126*
3.75	100*	93	80*	70*	62	62	171*	135
4.00	110*	100*	90*	80*	70*	66	180*	144*
4.25	120*	105	90*	80*	70	70	189*	153*
4.50	120*	111	100*	90*	80*	74	207*	162*
4.75	130*	117	100*	90*	80*	80*	216*	171*
5.00	140*	123	110*	100*	90*	82	225*	180

36 " WIDE FABRIC

TEMPLATE CODES

YARDS	R73	R74	R75	R76	R77	R78	R79	R80
0.25	3	2	2	2	1	1	1	1
0.50	9	7*	7*	7*	3	3	3	3
0.75	15	14*	10	10	7*	7*	7*	7*
1.00	21	14	14	14	7	7	7	7
1.25	28*	21*	21*	18	14*	14*	9	9
1.50	30	28*	21*	21*	14*	14*	14*	14*
1.75	36	28*	28*	24	21*	21*	14*	14*
2.00	42	35*	28	28	21*	21*	21*	14
2.25	49*	42*	35*	32	28*	21*	21*	21*
2.50	56*	42*	42*	36	28*	28*	21*	21*
2.75	63*	49*	42*	38	35*	28*	28*	21*
3.00	63	56*	49*	42	35*	35*	28*	28*
3.25	70*	63*	49*	46	42*	35*	35*	28*
3.50	77*	63*	56*	50	42*	42*	35*	35*
3.75	84*	70*	63*	54	49*	42*	35*	35*
4.00	91*	77*	63*	56	49*	42*	42*	35*
4.25	91*	77*	70*	63*	56*	49*	42*	42*
4.50	98*	84*	70*	64	56*	49*	49*	42*
4.75	105*	91*	77*	70*	63*	56*	49*	42*
5.00	112*	91*	84*	72	63*	56*	49*	49*

45 " WIDE FABRIC

TEMPLATE CODES

YARDS	R73	R74	R75	R76	R77	R78	R79	R80
0.25	4	3	3	2	2	2	1	1
0.50	12	9	9	9*	6	6	3	3
0.75	20	18*	15	10	10	10	9*	9*
1.00	28	21	21	18*	14	14	9*	9*
1.25	36	27	27	18	18	18	9	9
1.50	40	36*	30	27*	20	20	18*	18*
1.75	48	36	36	27*	27*	27*	18*	18*
2.00	56	45*	42	36*	28	28	27*	18*
2.25	64	54*	48	36*	36*	32	27*	27*
2.50	72	54	54	45*	36	36	27*	27*
2.75	81*	63*	57	45*	45*	38	36*	27*
3.00	84	72*	63	54*	45*	45*	36*	36*
3.25	92	81*	69	54*	54*	46	45*	36*
3.50	100	81*	75	63*	54*	54*	45*	45*
3.75	108	90*	81	63*	63*	54	45*	45*
4.00	117*	99*	84	72*	63*	56	54*	45*
4.25	120	99*	90	81*	72*	63*	54*	54*
4.50	128	108*	96	81*	72*	64	63*	54*
4.75	136	117*	102	90*	81*	72*	63*	54*
5.00	144	117*	108	90*	81*	72	63*	63*

36 " WIDE FABRIC

TEMPLATE CODES

YARDS	R81	R82	R83	R84	R85	R86	R87	R88
0.25	6*	6*	3	2	2	2	1	6*
0.50	15	12	9	6	6	6	3	12
0.75	20	18*	12	8	8	8	6*	18*
1.00	30	24	18	12	12	12	6	24
1.25	40	32	24	18*	16	16	12*	30*
1.50	45	36	30*	18	18	18	12*	42*
1.75	55	44	36*	24*	22	22	18*	48*
2.00	65	52	42*	26	26	26	18*	54*
2.25	70	56	48*	30*	30*	28	24*	60*
2.50	80	64	54*	36*	32	32	24*	66*
2.75	90	72	54	36	36	36	30*	72*
3.00	95	76	60*	42*	38	38	30*	84*
3.25	105	84	66*	48*	42	42	36*	90*
3.50	110	88	72*	48*	44	44	36*	96*
3.75	120	96	78*	54*	48	48	42*	102*
4.00	130	104	84*	54*	54*	52	42*	108*
4.25	135	108	90*	60*	54	54	48*	114*
4.50	145	116	96*	66*	60*	58	48*	126*
4.75	155	124	102*	66*	62	62	54*	132*
5.00	160	128	108*	72*	66*	64	54*	138*

45 " WIDE FABRIC

TEMPLATE CODES

YARDS	R81	R82	R83	R84	R85	R86	R87	R88
0.25	8*	8*	4	3	2	2	2	7*
0.50	18	16*	12	9	8*	8*	6	15
0.75	24	24*	16	12	8	8	8	21*
1.00	40*	32*	24	18	16*	16*	12	30
1.25	48	40	32	24	16	16	16	35
1.50	56*	48*	40*	27	24*	24*	18	49*
1.75	72*	56*	48*	33	24*	24*	24*	56*
2.00	80*	65	56*	39	32*	32*	26	63*
2.25	88*	72*	64*	42	40*	32*	32*	70*
2.50	96	80	72*	48	40*	40*	32	77*
2.75	112*	90	72	54	48*	40*	40*	84*
3.00	120*	96*	80*	57	48*	48*	40*	98*
3.25	128*	105	88*	64*	56*	48*	48*	105*
3.50	144*	112*	96*	66	56*	56*	48*	112*
3.75	152*	120	104*	72	64*	56*	56*	119*
4.00	160*	130	112*	78	72*	64*	56*	126*
4.25	168*	144*	120*	81	72*	64*	64*	133*
4.50	184*	152*	128*	88*	80*	72*	64*	147*
4.75	192*	160*	136*	93	80*	72*	72*	154*
5.00	200*	168*	144*	96	88*	80*	72*	161*

36 " WIDE FABRIC

TEMPLATE CODES

YARDS	R89	R90	R91	R92	R93	R94	R95	R96
0.25	3	3	2	2	1	1	5*	5*
0.50	9	9	6	6	3	3	10*	10*
0.75	12	12	8	8	6*	6*	15*	15*
1.00	18	18	12	12	6	6	20	20
1.25	24*	24*	14	14	12*	12*	25*	25*
1.50	30*	27	18	18	12*	12*	30*	30*
1.75	36*	30	20	20	18*	18*	36	36
2.00	42*	36	24	24	18*	18*	40	40
2.25	48*	42*	30*	26	24*	18*	45*	45*
2.50	54*	48*	30	30	24*	24*	50*	50*
2.75	60*	54*	36*	32	30*	24*	56	56
3.00	66*	54	36	36	30*	30*	60	60
3.25	72*	60*	42*	38	36*	30*	65*	65*
3.50	78*	66*	42	42	36*	36*	72	72
3.75	84*	72*	48*	44	36*	36*	76	76
4.00	90*	78*	54*	48	42*	36*	80	80
4.25	96*	78*	54*	50	42*	42*	90*	85*
4.50	102*	84*	60*	54	48*	42*	95*	92
4.75	108*	90*	60*	56	48*	48*	100*	96
5.00	114*	96*	66*	60	54*	48*	105*	100

45 " WIDE FABRIC

TEMPLATE CODES

YARDS	R89	R90	R91	R92	R93	R94	R95	R96
0.25	4	4	2	2	2	2	6*	6*
0.50	12	12	7*	7*	6	6	12*	12*
0.75	16	16	8	8	8	8	18*	18*
1.00	24	24	14*	14*	12	12	25	25
1.25	28	28	14	14	14	14	30	30
1.50	36	36	21*	21*	18	18	36*	36*
1.75	42*	40	21*	21*	21*	21*	45	45
2.00	49*	48	28*	28*	24	24	50	50
2.25	56*	52	35*	28*	28*	26	55	55
2.50	63*	60	35*	35*	30	30	60	60
2.75	70*	64	42*	35*	35*	32	70	70
3.00	77*	72	42*	42*	36	36	75	75
3.25	84*	76	49*	42*	42*	38	80	80
3.50	91*	84	49*	49*	42	42	90	90
3.75	98*	88	56*	49*	44	44	95	95
4.00	105*	96	63*	56*	49*	48	100	100
4.25	112*	100	63*	56*	50	50	108*	105
4.50	119*	108	70*	63*	56*	54	115	115
4.75	126*	112	70*	63*	56	56	120	120
5.00	133*	120	77*	70*	63*	60	126*	125

36 " WIDE FABRIC

YARDS	R97	R98	R99	R100	R101	R102	R103	R104
0.25	3	3	3	2	2	1	1	1
0.50	6	6	6	5*	5*	2	2	2
0.75	10*	10*	10*	10*	6	5*	5*	5*
1.00	15	15	15	10	10	5	5	5
1.25	20*	20*	18	15*	12	10*	10*	6
1.50	25*	21	21	20*	15*	10*	10*	10*
1.75	30*	27	27	20*	18	15*	15*	10*
2.00	35*	30	30	25*	20	15*	15*	15*
2.25	40*	35*	35*	30*	25*	20*	15*	15*
2.50	45*	40*	36	30*	25*	20*	20*	15*
2.75	45*	45*	42	35*	30*	25*	20*	20*
3.00	50*	45	45	40*	30	25*	25*	20*
3.25	55*	50*	50*	45*	35*	30*	25*	25*
3.50	60*	55*	54	45*	36	30*	30*	25*
3.75	65*	60*	57	50*	40*	35*	30*	25*
4.00	70*	65*	60	55*	45*	35*	30*	30*
4.25	75*	65*	65*	55*	45*	40*	35*	30*
4.50	80*	70*	70*	60*	50*	40*	35*	35*
4.75	85*	75*	72	65*	50*	45*	40*	35*
5.00	90*	80*	75	65*	55*	45*	40*	35*

45 " WIDE FABRIC

YARDS	R97	R98	R99	R100	R101	R102	R103	R104
0.25	4	4	3	3	2	2	2	1
0.50	8	8	6	6	6*	4	4	2
0.75	12	12	12*	12*	6	6	6	6*
1.00	20	20	18*	15	12*	10	10	6*
1.25	24	24	18	18	12	12	12	6
1.50	30*	28	24*	24*	18*	14	14	12*
1.75	36	36	30*	27	18	18	18	12*
2.00	42*	40	36*	30	24*	20	20	18*
2.25	48*	44	42*	36*	30*	24*	22	18*
2.50	54*	48	42*	36	30*	24	24	18*
2.75	56	56	48*	42	36*	30*	28	24*
3.00	60	60	54*	48*	36*	30	30	24*
3.25	66*	64	60*	54*	42*	36*	32	30*
3.50	72	72	60*	54	42*	36	36	30*
3.75	78*	76	66*	60*	48*	42*	38	30*
4.00	84*	80	72*	66*	54*	42*	40	36*
4.25	90*	84	78*	66*	54*	48*	42	36*
4.50	96*	92	84*	72*	60*	48*	46	42*
4.75	102*	96	84*	78*	60*	54*	48	42*
5.00	108*	100	90*	78*	66*	54*	50	42*

36" WIDE FABRIC

TEMPLATE CODES

YARDS	R105	R106	R107	R108	R109	R110	R111	R112
0.25	1	3	3	2	2	2	1	3
0.50	2	6	6	4	4	4	2	6
0.75	5*	9	9	8*	6	6	4*	9
1.00	5	12	12	8	8	8	4	12
1.25	6	16*	16*	12*	12*	10	8*	16*
1.50	10*	21	21	16*	14	14	8*	20*
1.75	10*	24	24	16	16	16	12*	24*
2.00	10	28*	27	20*	20*	18	12*	28*
2.25	15*	32*	30	24*	20	20	12*	32*
2.50	15*	36*	33	28*	24*	22	16*	36*
2.75	15*	40*	36	28*	24	24	16*	36*
3.00	20*	44*	42	32*	28	28	20*	40*
3.25	20*	48*	45	36*	32*	30	20*	44*
3.50	25*	52*	48	36*	32	32	24*	48*
3.75	25*	56*	51	40*	36*	34	24*	52*
4.00	25*	60*	54	44*	40*	36	24*	56*
4.25	30*	64*	57	48*	40*	38	28*	60*
4.50	30*	68*	63	48*	44*	42	28*	64*
4.75	30*	72*	66	52*	44	44	32*	68*
5.00	35*	76*	69	56*	48*	46	32*	72*

45 " WIDE FABRIC

TEMPLATE CODES

YARDS	R105	R106	R107	R108	R109	R110	R111	R112
0.25	1	4	4	3	3	2	2	4
0.50	2	8	8	6	6	5*	4	8
0.75	6*	12	12	10*	9	6	6	12
1.00	6*	16	16	12	12	10*	8	16
1.25	6	20	20	15	15	10	10	20
1.50	12*	28	28	21	21	15*	14	25*
1.75	12*	32	32	24	24	16	16	30*
2.00	12*	36	36	27	27	20*	18	35*
2.25	18*	40	40	30	30	20	20	40*
2.50	18*	45*	44	35*	33	25*	22	45*
2.75	18*	50*	48	36	36	25*	24	45*
3.00	24*	56	56	42	42	30*	28	50*
3.25	24*	60	60	45	45	30	30	55*
3.50	30*	65*	64	48	48	35*	32	60*
3.75	30*	70*	68	51	51	35*	34	65*
4.00	30*	75*	72	55*	54	40*	36	70*
4.25	36*	80*	76	60*	57	40*	38	75*
4.50	36*	85*	84	63	63	45*	42	80*
4.75	36*	90*	88	66	66	45*	44	85*
5.00	42*	95*	92	70*	69	50*	46	90*

36 " WIDE FABRIC

TEMPLATE CODES

YARDS	R113	R114	R115	R116	R117	R118	R119	R120
0.25	3	3	2	2	2	1	1	0
0.50	6	6	4	4	4	2	2	3
0.75	9	9	8*	6	6	4*	4*	6
1.00	12	12	8	8	8	4	4	9
1.25	15	16*	12*	12*	10	8*	5	12
1.50	18	18	16*	12	12	8*	8*	15
1.75	21	21	16*	16*	14	12*	8*	18
2.00	24	24	20*	16	16	12*	8	21
2.25	28*	28*	24*	20*	18	12*	12*	24
2.50	30	32*	24*	24*	20	16*	12*	27
2.75	33	36*	28*	24*	22	16*	12*	30
3.00	36	36	32*	28*	24	20*	16*	33
3.25	40*	40*	36*	28*	26	20*	16*	36
3.50	42	44*	36*	32*	28	24*	20*	39
3.75	45	48*	40*	36*	30	24*	20*	42
4.00	48	52*	44*	36*	32	24*	20*	45
4.25	54	52*	44*	40*	36*	28*	24*	48
4.50	57	56*	48*	40*	36	28*	24*	51
4.75	60	60*	52*	44*	40*	32*	24*	54
5.00	63	64*	52*	48*	40	32*	28*	57

45 " WIDE FABRIC

TEMPLATE CODES

YARDS	R113	R114	R115	R116	R117	R118	R119	R120
0.25	3	4	3	3	2	2	1	0
0.50	6	8	6	6	5*	4	2	4
0.75	10*	12	10*	9	6	6	5*	8
1.00	15*	16	12	12	10*	8	5*	12
1.25	15	20	15	15	10	10	5	16
1.50	20*	24	20*	18	15*	12	10*	20
1.75	25*	28	21	21	15*	15*	10*	24
2.00	30*	32	25*	24	20*	16	10*	28
2.25	35*	36	30*	27	20*	18	15*	32
2.50	35*	40	30	30	25*	20	15*	36
2.75	40*	45*	35*	33	25*	22	15*	40
3.00	45*	48	40*	36	30*	25*	20*	44
3.25	50*	52	45*	39	30*	26	20*	48
3.50	50*	56	45*	42	35*	30*	25*	52
3.75	55*	60	50*	45	35*	30	25*	56
4.00	60*	65*	55*	48	40*	32	25*	60
4.25	65*	68	55*	51	45*	35*	30*	64
4.50	70*	72	60*	54	45*	36	30*	68
4.75	70*	76	65*	57	50*	40*	30*	72
5.00	75*	80	65*	60	50*	40	35*	76

36 " WIDE FABRIC

TEMPLATE CODES

YARDS	R121	R122	R123	R124	R125	R126	R127	R128
0.25	0	0	0	0	0	0	0	0
0.50	3*	3*	3*	1	3*	3*	3*	1
0.75	6*	6*	4	3*	6*	4	4	3*
1.00	6	6	6	3	6	6	6	3
1.25	9*	9*	8	6*	9*	9*	9*	6*
1.50	12*	12*	10	6*	12*	9*	9*	6*
1.75	12	12	12	9*	12*	12*	12*	9*
2.00	15*	15*	14	9*	15*	15*	12	9*
2.25	18*	18*	16	12*	18*	15*	15*	12*
2.50	21*	18	18	12*	18*	18*	18*	12*
2.75	21*	21*	18	15*	21*	18	18	15*
3.00	24*	24*	20	15*	24*	21*	21*	15*
3.25	27*	27*	22	18*	27*	24*	21*	18*
3.50	27*	27*	24	18*	27*	24*	24*	18*
3.75	30*	30*	26	21*	30*	27*	27*	18*
4.00	33*	33*	28	21*	33*	30*	27*	21*
4.25	36*	33*	30	24*	33*	30*	30*	21*
4.50	36*	36*	32	24*	36*	33*	30*	24*
4.75	39*	39*	34	27*	39*	33*	33*	24*
5.00	42*	39*	36	27*	39*	36*	36*	27*

45 " WIDE FABRIC

TEMPLATE CODES

YARDS	R121	R122	R123	R124	R125	R126	R127	R128
0.25	0	0	0	0	0	0	0	0
0.50	4*	4*	4*	2	4*	4*	4*	2
0.75	8*	8*	4	4	8*	6	6	4
1.00	9	9	8*	6	9	9	9	6
1.25	12	12	8	8	12	12	12	8
1.50	16*	16*	12*	10	16*	12	12	8
1.75	18	18	12	12	16*	16*	16*	12*
2.00	21	21	16*	14	20*	20*	18	12
2.25	24	24	16	16	24*	21	21	16*
2.50	28*	27	20*	18	24	24	24	16
2.75	30	28*	20*	20*	28*	27	27	20*
3.00	33	32*	24*	20	32*	28*	28*	20*
3.25	36	36*	24*	24*	36*	32*	30	24*
3.50	39	36	28*	24	36*	33	33	24*
3.75	42	40*	28*	28*	40*	36	36	24
4.00	45	44*	32*	28	44*	40*	39	28*
4.25	48	45	32*	32*	44*	40*	40*	28*
4.50	51	48	36*	32	48*	44*	42	32*
4.75	54	52*	36*	36*	52*	45	45	32*
5.00	57	54	40*	36	52*	48	48	36*

36 " WIDE FABRIC

YARDS	R129	R130	R131	R132	R133	R134	R135	R136
0.25	0	0	0	0	0	0	0	0
0.50	1	3*	1	2	1	2	1	1
0.75	3*	4	3*	4	2	4	2	2
1.00	3	6	3	4	2	4	2	2
1.25	6*	6	6*	6	4*	6	4*	3
1.50	6*	9*	6*	8	4	8	4	4
1.75	9*	10	9*	8	6*	8	6*	4
2.00	9*	12	9*	10	6*	10	6*	6*
2.25	9*	15*	12*	12	6	12	8*	6
2.50	12*	15*	12*	14	8*	12	8*	6
2.75	12*	18*	15*	14	8*	14	10*	8*
3.00	15*	18	15*	16	10*	16	10*	8
3.25	15*	21*	18*	18	10*	18	12*	10*
3.50	18*	21*	18*	18	12*	18	12*	10*
3.75	18*	24*	21*	20	12*	20	14*	10
4.00	18*	27*	21*	22	12*	22	14*	12*
4.25	21*	27*	24*	24	14*	22	16*	12*
4.50	21*	30*	24*	24	14*	24	16*	14*
4.75	24*	30*	27*	26	16*	26	18*	14*
5.00	24*	33*	27*	28	16*	26	18*	14*

45 " WIDE FABRIC

YARDS	R129	R130	R131	R132	R133	R134	R135	R136
0.25	0	0	0	0	0	0	0	0
0.50	2	3*	2	3*	2	3*	2	1
0.75	4	4	4	4	4	4	4	3*
1.00	6	6	6	6*	4	6*	4	3*
1.25	8	6	6	6	6	6	6	3
1.50	8	9*	8	9*	8	9*	8	6*
1.75	12*	10	10	9*	9*	9*	9*	6*
2.00	12	12	12	12*	10	12*	10	9*
2.25	14	15*	14	12	12	12	12	9*
2.50	16	15*	14	15*	14	15*	12	9*
2.75	18	18*	16	15*	14	15*	15*	12*
3.00	20*	18	18	18*	16	18*	16	12*
3.25	20	21*	20	18	18	18	18	15*
3.50	24*	21*	20	21*	18	21*	18	15*
3.75	24	24*	22	21*	20	21*	21*	15*
4.00	26	27*	24	24*	22	24*	22	18*
4.25	28*	27*	26	24	24	27*	24*	18*
4.50	28	30*	28	27*	24	27*	24	21*
4.75	32*	30*	28	27*	26	30*	27*	21*
5.00	32	33*	30	30*	28	30*	27*	21*

36 " WIDE FABRIC

YARDS	R137	R138	R139	R140	R141
0.25	0	0	0	0	0
0.50	1	1	1	1	1
0.75	2	2*	2*	2*	2*
1.00	2	2	2	2	2
1.25	3	4*	4*	3	2
1.50	4	4*	4*	4*	4*
1.75	4	6*	6*	4	4*
2.00	5	6*	6*	4	4
2.25	6	6*	6*	6*	6*
2.50	6	8*	8*	6	6*
2.75	7	8*	8*	6	6*
3.00	8	10*	10*	8*	8*
3.25	9	10*	10*	8*	8*
3.50	10*	12*	12*	10*	10*
3.75	10	12*	12*	10*	10*
4.00	11	12*	12*	10*	10*
4.25	12*	14*	14*	12*	12*
4.50	12	14*	14*	12*	12*
4.75	13	16*	16*	12*	12*
5.00	14*	16*	16*	14*	14*

Header: TEMPLATE CODES

45 " WIDE FABRIC

YARDS	R137	R138	R139	R140	R141
0.25	0	0	0	0	0
0.50	1	2	2	1	1
0.75	3*	3*	3*	3*	2*
1.00	3*	4	4	3*	2
1.25	3	6	6	3	2
1.50	6*	6	6	6*	4*
1.75	6*	9*	9*	6*	4*
2.00	6*	10	9*	6*	4
2.25	9*	10	10	9*	6*
2.50	9*	12	12	9*	6*
2.75	9*	12	12	9*	6*
3.00	12*	15*	15*	12*	8*
3.25	12*	16	15*	12*	8*
3.50	15*	18*	18*	15*	10*
3.75	15*	18	18	15*	10*
4.00	15*	20	18	15*	10*
4.25	18*	21*	21*	18*	12*
4.50	18*	22	21*	18*	12*
4.75	18*	24*	24*	18*	12*
5.00	21*	24	24	21*	14*

Header: TEMPLATE CODES

Triangle Template Measurements and Codes

Code	Measurement	Notes
T1	1½″ × 1½″	
T2	1⅔″ × 1⅔″	
T3	2″ × 2″	
T4	2⅛″ × 2⅛″	¼ of 3″ square
T5	2⅜″ × 2⅜″	¼ of 3⅓″ square
T6	2¾″ × 2¾″	¼ of 4″ square
T7	3″ × 3″	
T8	3³⁄₁₆″ × 3³⁄₁₆″	¼ of 4½″ square
T9	3⅓″ × 3⅓″	
T10	3½″ × 3½″	¼ of 5″ square
T11	3″ × 4½″	
T12	3⅓″ × 5″	
T13	4″ × 4″	
T14	4¼″ × 4¼″	¼ of 6″ square
T15	4½″ × 4½″	
T16	4⅔″ × 4⅔″	¼ of 6⅔″ square
T17	4″ × 6″	
T18	4½″ × 6″	
T19	5″ × 5″	
T20	5⅝″ × 5⅝″	¼ of 8″ square
T21	5″ × 6⅔″	
T22	6″ × 6″	
T23	6⅜″ × 6⅜″	¼ of 9″ square
T24	6⅔″ × 6⅔″	
T25	6″ × 8″	
T26	7″ × 7″	¼ of 10″ square
T27	7½″ × 7½″	
T28	8″ × 8″	
T29	8⅓″ × 8⅓″	
T30	8½″ × 8½″	
T31	9″ × 9″	
T32	10″ × 10″	
T33	10½″ × 10½″	
T34	12″ × 12″	
T35	13⅓″ × 13⅓″	
T36	16″ × 16″	
T37	11⅔″ × 11⅔″	
T38	14″ × 14″	
T39	4½″ × 7½″	
T40	5″ × 8⅓″	
T41	6″ × 10″	
T42	2¼″ × 3¾″	
T43	2½″ × 4⅙″	
T44	3″ × 5″	

36 " WIDE FABRIC

TEMPLATE CODES

YARDS	T1	T2	T3	T4	T5	T6	T7	T8
0.25	44	40	36	36	32	32	14	14
0.50	110	100	72	72	64	64	42	42
0.75	176	160	126	126	96	96	70	70
1.00	242	200	162	162	128	128	98	98
1.25	308	260	216	198	176	160	126	126
1.50	352	320	252	252	208	192	154	154
1.75	418	360	288	288	240	224	182	168
2.00	484	420	342	324	272	256	210	196
2.25	550	480	378	378	304	288	238	224
2.50	616	520	432	414	352	320	266	252
2.75	660	580	468	450	384	352	294	280
3.00	726	640	522	504	416	384	308	308
3.25	792	680	558	540	448	416	336	322
3.50	858	740	594	576	480	448	364	350
3.75	924	800	648	630	528	480	392	378
4.00	968	840	684	666	560	512	420	406
4.25	1034	900	738	702	592	544	448	434
4.50	1100	960	774	756	624	576	476	462
4.75	1166	1000	828	792	656	608	504	476
5.00	1232	1060	864	828	704	640	532	504

45 " WIDE FABRIC

TEMPLATE CODES

YARDS	T1	T2	T3	T4	T5	T6	T7	T8
0.25	56	52	48	44	44	40	18	18
0.50	140	130	96	88	88	80	54	54
0.75	224	208	168	154	132	120	90	90
1.00	308	260	216	198	176	160	126	126
1.25	392	338	288	242	242	200	162	162
1.50	448	416	336	308	286	240	198	198
1.75	532	468	384	352	330	280	234	216
2.00	616	546	456	396	374	320	270	252
2.25	700	624	504	462	418	360	306	288
2.50	784	676	576	506	484	400	342	324
2.75	840	754	624	550	528	440	378	360
3.00	924	832	696	616	572	480	396	396
3.25	1008	884	744	660	616	520	432	414
3.50	1092	962	792	704	660	560	468	450
3.75	1176	1040	864	770	726	600	504	486
4.00	1232	1092	912	814	770	640	540	522
4.25	1316	1170	984	858	814	680	576	558
4.50	1400	1248	1032	924	858	720	612	594
4.75	1484	1300	1104	968	902	760	648	612
5.00	1568	1378	1152	1012	968	800	684	648

36 " WIDE FABRIC

TEMPLATE CODES

YARDS	T9	T10	T11	T12	T13	T14	T15	T16
0.25	14	12	20	14*	12	12	10	10
0.50	42	36	40	30	36	36	20	20
0.75	70	60	64*	50	48	48	40	40
1.00	98	72	80	70	72	72	50	50
1.25	112	96	100	90	84	84	70	70
1.50	140	120	128*	110	108	108	80	80
1.75	168	144	144*	130	132	120	100	90
2.00	196	156	160	150	144	144	110	110
2.25	224	180	192*	160	168	156	130	120
2.50	238	204	208*	180	180	180	140	140
2.75	266	228	224*	200	204	192	150	150
3.00	294	240	256*	220	216	216	170	160
3.25	322	264	272*	240	240	228	180	180
3.50	336	288	288*	260	264	252	200	190
3.75	364	300	320*	280	276	264	210	210
4.00	392	324	336*	300	300	288	230	220
4.25	420	348	368*	320	312	300	240	240
4.50	448	372	384*	330	336	324	260	250
4.75	462	384	400*	350	348	336	270	260
5.00	490	408	432*	370	372	360	280	280

45 " WIDE FABRIC

TEMPLATE CODES

YARDS	T9	T10	T11	T12	T13	T14	T15	T16
0.25	16	16	24	18*	14	14	14	14
0.50	48	48	48	36	42	42	28	28
0.75	80	80	80*	60	56	56	56	56
1.00	112	96	100*	90*	84	84	70	70
1.25	128	128	120	108	98	98	98	98
1.50	160	160	160*	132	126	126	112	112
1.75	192	192	180*	156	154	140	140	126
2.00	224	208	200*	180	168	168	154	154
2.25	256	240	240*	198*	196	182	182	168
2.50	272	272	260*	216	210	210	196	196
2.75	304	304	280*	240	238	224	210	210
3.00	336	320	320*	270*	252	252	238	224
3.25	368	352	340*	288	280	266	252	252
3.50	384	384	360*	312	308	294	280	266
3.75	416	400	400*	336	322	308	294	294
4.00	448	432	420*	360	350	336	322	308
4.25	480	464	460*	384	364	350	336	336
4.50	512	496	480*	396	392	378	364	350
4.75	528	512	500*	420	406	392	378	364
5.00	560	544	540*	450*	434	420	392	392

36 " WIDE FABRIC

YARDS	T17	T18	T19	T20	T21	T22	T23	T24
0.25	12*	12*	10	8	10*	8	8	8
0.50	24	24	20	16	20*	16	16	16
0.75	36*	36*	40	24	32	24	24	24
1.00	48	48	50	32	40	32	32	32
1.25	64	60*	60	48	50*	40	40	40
1.50	72	72	80	56	64	56	48	48
1.75	88	84*	90	64	72	64	56	56
2.00	104	108*	100	72	88	72	64	64
2.25	112	120*	120	88	96	80	80	72
2.50	132*	132*	130	96	104	88	88	80
2.75	144	144*	140	104	120	96	96	88
3.00	156*	156*	160	112	128	112	104	96
3.25	168	168*	170	120	144	120	112	104
3.50	184	180*	180	136	152	128	120	120
3.75	192	192*	200	144	160	136	128	128
4.00	208	216*	210	152	176	144	136	136
4.25	224	228*	220	160	184	152	144	144
4.50	232	240*	240	176	192	168	160	152
4.75	248	252*	250	184	208	176	168	160
5.00	264	264*	260	192	216	184	176	168

45 " WIDE FABRIC

YARDS	T17	T18	T19	T20	T21	T22	T23	T24
0.25	16*	14*	12	12	12*	10	10	10
0.50	32*	30	24	24	24*	20	20	20
0.75	48*	42*	48	36	40	30	30	30
1.00	64*	60	60	48	50	40	40	40
1.25	80	70	72	72	60	50	50	50
1.50	96*	90	96	84	80	70	60	60
1.75	112*	100	108	96	90	80	70	70
2.00	130	126*	120	108	110	90	80	80
2.25	144*	140*	144	132	120	100	100	90
2.50	176*	154*	156	144	130	110	110	100
2.75	192*	168*	168	156	150	120	120	110
3.00	208*	182*	192	168	160	140	130	120
3.25	224*	196*	204	180	180	150	140	130
3.50	240*	210	216	204	190	160	150	150
3.75	256*	224*	240	216	200	170	160	160
4.00	272*	252*	252	228	220	180	170	170
4.25	288*	266*	264	240	230	190	180	180
4.50	304*	280*	288	264	240	210	200	190
4.75	320*	294*	300	276	260	220	210	200
5.00	352*	308*	312	288	270	230	220	210

36 " WIDE FABRIC

TEMPLATE CODES

YARDS	T25	T26	T27	T28	T29	T30	T31	T32
0.25	6	8	0	0	0	0	0	0
0.50	12	16	6	6	6	6	6	6
0.75	18	24	12	12	12	12	12	12
1.00	24	32	18	18	18	18	18	18
1.25	36	40	24	24	24	24	24	18
1.50	42	48	30	30	30	30	30	24
1.75	48	56	36	36	36	36	30	30
2.00	56*	64	42	42	42	42	36	36
2.25	64*	72	48	48	48	42	42	36
2.50	72	80	54	54	48	48	48	42
2.75	78	88	60	60	54	54	54	48
3.00	84	96	66	66	60	60	60	54
3.25	90	104	72	72	66	66	60	54
3.50	96	112	78	72	72	72	66	60
3.75	108	120	84	78	78	78	72	66
4.00	114	128	90	84	84	84	78	72
4.25	120	136	96	90	90	84	84	78
4.50	128*	144	102	96	96	90	90	78
4.75	136*	152	108	102	102	96	90	84
5.00	144	160	114	108	102	102	96	90

45 " WIDE FABRIC

TEMPLATE CODES

YARDS	T25	T26	T27	T28	T29	T30	T31	T32
0.25	8	10	0	0	0	0	0	0
0.50	16	20	8	8	8	8	8	6
0.75	24	30	16	16	16	16	16	12
1.00	36*	40	24	24	24	24	24	18
1.25	48	50	32	32	32	32	32	18
1.50	60*	60	40	40	40	40	40	24
1.75	72*	70	48	48	48	48	40	30
2.00	84*	80	56	56	56	56	48	36
2.25	96*	90	64	64	64	56	56	36
2.50	108*	100	72	72	64	64	64	42
2.75	108*	110	80	80	72	72	72	48
3.00	120*	120	88	88	80	80	80	54
3.25	132*	130	96	96	88	88	80	54
3.50	144*	140	104	96	96	96	88	60
3.75	156*	150	112	104	104	104	96	66
4.00	168*	160	120	112	112	112	104	72
4.25	180*	170	128	120	120	112	112	78
4.50	192*	180	136	128	128	120	120	78
4.75	204*	190	144	136	136	128	120	84
5.00	216*	200	152	144	136	136	128	90

36 " WIDE FABRIC

TEMPLATE CODES

YARDS	T33	T34	T35	T36	T37	T38	T39	T40
0.25	0	0	0	0	0	0	6	6
0.50	4	4	4	4	4	4	18	12
0.75	8	4	4	4	8	4	24	24
1.00	8	8	8	8	8	8	36	30
1.25	12	12	8	8	12	8	48*	42
1.50	16	12	12	12	16	12	60*	50*
1.75	20	16	16	12	16	16	72*	54
2.00	20	20	16	16	20	16	84*	66
2.25	24	20	20	16	24	20	96*	72
2.50	28	24	20	20	24	20	108*	84
2.75	32	28	24	20	28	24	120*	90
3.00	32	28	28	24	32	24	132*	100*
3.25	36	32	28	24	32	28	132*	108
3.50	40	36	32	28	36	32	144*	114
3.75	44	36	32	28	40	32	156*	126
4.00	44	40	36	32	40	36	168*	132
4.25	48	44	40	32	44	36	180*	140*
4.50	52	44	40	36	48	40	192*	150
4.75	56	48	44	36	48	40	204*	160*
5.00	56	52	44	40	52	44	216*	168

45 " WIDE FABRIC

TEMPLATE CODES

YARDS	T33	T34	T35	T36	T37	T38	T39	T40
0.25	0	0	0	0	0	0	8	8
0.50	6	6	4	4	6	4	24	16
0.75	12	6	4	4	12	4	32	32
1.00	12	12	8	8	12	8	48	42*
1.25	18	18	8	8	18	8	56	56
1.50	24	18	12	12	24	12	72	70*
1.75	30	24	16	12	24	16	84*	72
2.00	30	30	16	16	30	16	98*	88
2.25	36	30	20	16	36	20	112*	98*
2.50	42	36	20	20	36	20	126*	112
2.75	48	42	24	20	42	24	140*	126*
3.00	48	42	28	24	48	24	154*	140*
3.25	54	48	28	24	48	28	154*	144
3.50	60	54	32	28	54	32	168	154*
3.75	66	54	32	28	60	32	182*	168
4.00	66	60	36	32	60	36	196*	182*
4.25	72	66	40	32	66	36	210*	196*
4.50	78	66	40	36	72	40	224*	210*
4.75	84	72	44	36	72	40	238*	224*
5.00	84	78	44	40	78	44	252*	224

36 " WIDE FABRIC

			TEMPLATE CODES	
YARDS	T41	T42	T43	T44
0.25	4	20	20	16
0.50	8	40	40	32
0.75	16*	72*	72*	48
1.00	16	90	90	64
1.25	24	126*	110	96*
1.50	32*	144*	144*	112*
1.75	40*	180*	162*	128*
2.00	40*	198*	198*	144*
2.25	48*	234*	216*	176*
2.50	56*	252*	234*	192*
2.75	64*	288*	270*	208*
3.00	64*	306*	288*	224*
3.25	72*	342*	324*	256*
3.50	80*	360*	342*	272*
3.75	80*	396*	360*	288*
4.00	88*	414*	396*	304*
4.25	96*	450*	414*	320*
4.50	104*	468*	450*	352*
4.75	104*	504*	468*	368*
5.00	112*	522*	486*	384*

45 " WIDE FABRIC

			TEMPLATE CODES	
YARDS	T41	T42	T43	T44
0.25	6	28	24	24
0.50	12	56	48	48
0.75	24*	98	88*	72
1.00	24	126	110*	96
1.25	36	168	132	120
1.50	48*	196	176*	144
1.75	60*	240*	198*	168
2.00	60*	266	242*	192
2.25	72*	312*	264*	220*
2.50	84*	336	286*	240
2.75	96*	384*	330*	264
3.00	96*	408*	352*	288
3.25	108*	456*	396*	320*
3.50	120*	480*	418*	340*
3.75	120*	528*	440*	360
4.00	132*	552*	484*	384
4.25	144*	600*	506*	408
4.50	156*	624*	550*	440*
4.75	156*	672*	572*	468
5.00	168*	696*	594*	492